The *New* Daily Study Bible

The Letters to the
Galatians and Ephesians

The *New* Daily Study Bible

The Letters to the
Galatians and Ephesians

William Barclay

Westminster John Knox Press
LOUISVILLE • LONDON

© The William Barclay Estate, 1976, 2002

First editions published in 1954 as *The Daily Study Bible: The Letter to the Galatians* and in 1956 as *The Daily Study Bible: The Letter to the Ephesians*
Revised edition published in 1976
This third edition fully revised and updated by Saint Andrew Press and published as *The New Daily Study Bible: The Letters to the Galatians and Ephesians* in 2002

Published in the United States by
Westminster John Knox Press
Louisville, Kentucky

The Scripture quotations contained herein are from The New Revised Standard Version of the Bible, Anglicized Edition, copyright © 1989, 1995 by the Division of Christian Education of the National Council of the Churches of Christ in the United States of America, and are used by permission. All rights reserved.

The right of William Barclay to be identified as author of this work has been asserted according to the Copyright, Designs and Patents Act, 1988.

Cover design by McColl Productions Ltd, by courtesy of Saint Andrew Press

Typeset by Waverley Typesetters, Galashiels

PRINTED IN THE UNITED STATES OF AMERICA

02 03 04 05 06 07 08 09 10 11 — 10 9 8 7 6 5 4 3 2 1

Library of Congress Cataloging-in-Publication Data is on file at the Library of Congress, Washington, D.C.

ISBN 0-664-22559-4

To

ALL THE STUDENTS OF TRINITY COLLEGE

WHOM IT HAS BEEN MY PRIVILEGE TO TEACH

AND WHO ARE NOW ENGAGED UPON THE WORK

OF THE CHURCH AT HOME

AND

OF THE YOUNGER CHURCHES OVERSEAS

CONTENTS

GALATIANS AND EPHESIANS

EPHESIANS

SERIES FOREWORD
(by Ronnie Barclay)

My father always had a great love for the English language and its literature. As a student at the University of Glasgow, he won a prize in the English class – and I have no doubt that he could have become a Professor of English instead of Divinity and Biblical Criticism. In a pre-computer age, he had a mind like a computer that could store vast numbers of quotations, illustrations, anecdotes and allusions; and, more remarkably still, he could retrieve them at will. The editor of this revision has, where necessary, corrected and attributed the vast majority of these quotations with considerable skill and has enhanced our pleasure as we read quotations from Plato to T. S. Eliot.

There is another very welcome improvement in the new text. My mother was one of five sisters, and my grandmother was a commanding figure as the Presbyterian minister's wife in a small village in Ayrshire in Scotland. She ran that small community very efficiently, and I always felt that my father, surrounded by so many women, was more than somewhat overawed by it all! I am sure that this is the reason why his use of English tended to be dominated by the words 'man', 'men' and so on, with the result that it sounded very male-orientated. Once again, the editor has very skilfully improved my father's English and made the text much more readable for all of us by amending the often one-sided language.

It is a well-known fact that William Barclay wrote at breakneck speed and never corrected anything once it was on paper – he took great pride in mentioning this at every possible opportunity! This revision, in removing repetition and correcting the inevitable errors that had slipped through, has produced a text free from all the tell-tale signs of very rapid writing. It is with great pleasure that I commend this revision to readers old and new in the certainty that William Barclay speaks even more clearly to us all with his wonderful appeal in this new version of his much-loved *Daily Study Bible*.

Ronnie Barclay
Bedfordshire
2001

GENERAL INTRODUCTION

(by William Barclay, from the 1975 edition)

The Daily Study Bible series has always had one aim – to convey the results of scholarship to the ordinary reader. A. S. Peake delighted in the saying that he was a 'theological middle-man', and I would be happy if the same could be said of me in regard to these volumes. And yet the primary aim of the series has never been academic. It could be summed up in the famous words of Richard of Chichester's prayer – to enable men and women 'to know Jesus Christ more clearly, to love him more dearly, and to follow him more nearly'.

It is all of twenty years since the first volume of *The Daily Study Bible* was published. The series was the brain-child of the late Rev. Andrew McCosh, MA, STM, the then Secretary and Manager of the Committee on Publications of the Church of Scotland, and of the late Rev. R. G. Macdonald, OBE, MA, DD, its Convener.

It is a great joy to me to know that all through the years *The Daily Study Bible* has been used at home and abroad, by minister, by missionary, by student and by layman, and that it has been translated into many different languages. Now, after so many printings, it has become necessary to renew the printer's type and the opportunity has been taken to restyle the books, to correct some errors in the text and to remove some references which have become outdated. At the same time, the Biblical quotations within the text have been changed to use the Revised Standard Version, but my own original translation of the New Testament passages has been retained at the beginning of each daily section.

There is one debt which I would be sadly lacking in courtesy if I did not acknowledge. The work of revision and correction has been done entirely by the Rev. James Martin, MA, BD, Minister of High Carntyne Church, Glasgow. Had it not been for him this task would never have been undertaken, and it is impossible for me to thank him enough for the selfless toil he has put into the revision of these books.

It is my prayer that God may continue to use *The Daily Study Bible* to enable men better to understand His word.

William Barclay
Glasgow
1975
(Published in the 1975 edition)

GENERAL FOREWORD

(by John Drane)

I only met William Barclay once, not long after his retirement from the chair of Biblical Criticism at the University of Glasgow. Of course I had known about him long before that, not least because his theological passion – the Bible – was also a significant formative influence in my own life and ministry. One of my most vivid memories of his influence goes back to when I was working on my own doctoral research in the New Testament. It was summer 1971, and I was a leader on a mission team working in the north-east of Scotland at the same time as Barclay's Baird Lectures were being broadcast on national television. One night, a young Ph.D. scientist who was interested in Christianity, but still unsure about some things, came to me and announced: 'I've just been watching William Barclay on TV. He's convinced me that I need to be a Christian; when can I be baptized?' That kind of thing did not happen every day. So how could it be that Barclay's message was so accessible to people with no previous knowledge or experience of the Christian faith?

I soon realised that there was no magic ingredient that enabled this apparently ordinary professor to be a brilliant communicator. His secret lay in who he was, his own sense of identity and purpose, and above all his integrity in being true to himself and his faith. Born in the far north of Scotland, he was brought up in Motherwell, a steel-producing town south of Glasgow where his family settled when he was only five, and this was the kind of place where he felt most at home. Though his association with the University of Glasgow provided a focus for his life over almost fifty years, from his first day as a student in 1925 to his retirement from the faculty in 1974, he never became an ivory-tower academic, divorced from the realities of life in the real world. On the contrary, it was his commitment to the working-class culture of industrial Clydeside that enabled him to make such a lasting contribution not only to the world of the university but also to the life of the Church.

He was ordained to the ministry of the Church of Scotland at the age of twenty-six, but was often misunderstood even by other Christians. I doubt that William Barclay would ever have chosen words such as 'missionary' or 'evangelist' to describe his own ministry, but he accomplished what few others have done, as he took the traditional Presbyterian emphasis on spirituality-through-learning and transformed it into a most effective vehicle for evangelism. His own primary interest was in the history and language of the New Testament, but William Barclay was never only a historian or literary critic. His constant concern was to explore how these ancient books, and the faith of which they spoke, could continue to be relevant to people of his own time. If the Scottish churches had known how to capitalize on his enormous popularity in the media during the 1960s and 1970s, they might easily have avoided much of the decline of subsequent years.

Connecting the Bible to life has never been the way to win friends in the world of academic theology, and Barclay could undoubtedly have made things easier for himself had he been prepared to be a more conventional academic. But he was too deeply rooted in his own culture – and too seriously committed to the gospel – for that. He could see little purpose in a belief system that was so wrapped up in arcane and complicated terminology that it was accessible only to experts. Not only did he demystify Christian theology, but he also did it for working people, addressing the kind of things that mattered to ordinary folks in their everyday lives. In doing so, he also challenged the elitism that has often been deeply ingrained in the twin worlds of academic theology and the Church, with their shared assumption that popular culture is an inappropriate vehicle for serious thinking. Professor Barclay can hardly have been surprised when his predilection for writing books for the masses – not to mention talking to them on television – was questioned by his peers and even occasionally dismissed as being 'unscholarly' or insufficiently 'academic'. That was all untrue, of course, for his work was soundly based in reliable scholarship and his own extensive knowledge of the original languages of the Bible. But like One many centuries before him (and unlike most of his peers, in both Church and academy), 'the common people heard him gladly' (Mark 12:37), which no doubt explains why his writings are still inspirational – and why it is a particular pleasure for me personally to commend them to a new readership in a new century.

John Drane
University of Aberdeen
2001

EDITOR'S PREFACE

(by Linda Foster)

When the first volume of the original *Daily Bible Readings*, which later became *The Daily Study Bible* (the commentary on Acts), was published in 1953, no one could have anticipated or envisaged the revolution in the use of language which was to take place in the last quarter of the twentieth century. Indeed, when the first revised edition, to which William Barclay refers in his General Introduction, was completed in 1975, such a revolution was still waiting in the wings. But at the beginning of the twenty-first century, inclusive language and the concept of political correctness are well-established facts of life. It has therefore been with some trepidation that the editing of this unique and much-loved text has been undertaken in producing *The New Daily Study Bible*. Inevitably, the demands of the new language have resulted in the loss of some of Barclay's most sonorous phrases, perhaps best remembered in the often-repeated words 'many a man'. Nonetheless, this revision is made in the conviction that William Barclay, the great communicator, would have welcomed it. In the discussion of Matthew 9:16–17 ('The Problem of the New Idea'), he affirmed the value of language that has stood the test of time and in which people have 'found comfort and put their trust', but he also spoke of 'living in a changing and expanding world' and questioned the wisdom of reading God's word to twentieth-century men and women in Elizabethan English. It is the intention of this new edition to heed that warning and to bring

William Barclay's message of God's word to readers of the twenty-first century in the language of their own time.

In the editorial process, certain decisions have been made in order to keep a balance between that new language and the familiar Barclay style. Quotations from the Bible are now taken from the New Revised Standard Version, but William Barclay's own translation of individual passages has been retained throughout. Where the new version differs from the text on which Barclay originally commented, because of the existence of an alternative reading, the variant text is indicated by square brackets. I have made no attempt to guess what Barclay would have said about the NRSV text; his commentary still refers to the Authorized (King James) and Revised Standard Versions of the Bible, but I believe that the inclusive language of the NRSV considerably assists the flow of the discussion.

For similar reasons, the dating conventions of BC and AD – rather than the more recent and increasingly used BCE (before the common era) and CE (common era) – have been retained. William Barclay took great care to explain the meanings of words and phrases and scholarly points, but it has not seemed appropriate to select new terms and make such explanations on his behalf.

One of the most difficult problems to solve has concerned monetary values. Barclay had his own system for translating the coinage of New Testament times into British currency. Over the years, these equivalent values have become increasingly out of date, and often the force of the point being made has been lost or diminished. There is no easy way to bring these equivalents up to date in a way that will continue to make sense, particularly when readers come from both sides of the Atlantic. I have therefore followed the only known yardstick that gives any feel for the values concerned, namely that a *denarius* was a day's wage for a working man, and I have made alterations to the text accordingly.

One of the striking features of *The Daily Study Bible* is the range of quotations from literature and hymnody that are used by way of illustration. Many of these passages appeared without identification or attribution, and for the new edition I have attempted wherever possible to provide sources and authors. In the same way, details have been included about scholars and other individuals cited, by way of context and explanation, and I am most grateful to Professor John Drane for his assistance in discovering information about some of the more obscure or unfamiliar characters. It is clear that readers use *The Daily Study Bible* in different ways. Some look up particular passages while others work through the daily readings in a more systematic way. The descriptions and explanations are therefore not offered every time an individual is mentioned (in order to avoid repetition that some may find tedious), but I trust that the information can be discovered without too much difficulty.

Finally, the 'Further Reading' lists at the end of each volume have been removed. Many new commentaries and individual studies have been added to those that were the basis of William Barclay's work, and making a selection from that ever-increasing catalogue is an impossible task. It is nonetheless my hope that the exploration that begins with these volumes of *The New Daily Study Bible* will go on in the discovery of new writers and new books.

Throughout the editorial process, many conversations have taken place – conversations with the British and American publishers, and with those who love the books and find in them both information and inspiration. Ronnie Barclay's contribution to this revision of his father's work has been invaluable. But one conversation has dominated the work, and that has been a conversation with William Barclay himself through the text. There has been a real sense of listening to his voice in all the questioning and in the searching for new words to convey the meaning of that text. The aim of *The New Daily Study Bible* is to make clear his message, so that the distinctive voice, which has spoken to so many in past years, may continue to be heard for generations to come.

Linda Foster
London
2001

A GENERAL INTRODUCTION
TO THE LETTERS OF PAUL

The Letters of Paul

There is no more interesting body of documents in the New Testament than the letters of Paul. That is because, of all forms of literature, a letter is most personal. Demetrius, one of the ancient Greek literary critics, once wrote: 'Everyone reveals his own soul in his letters. In every other form of composition it is possible to discern the writer's character, but in none so clearly as the epistolary' (Demetrius, *On Style*, 227). It is precisely because he left us so many letters that we feel we know Paul so well. In them, he opened his mind and heart to the people he loved so much; and in them, to this day, we can see that great mind grappling with the problems of the early Church, and feel that great heart throbbing with love for men and women, even when they were misguided and mistaken.

The Difficulty of Letters

At the same time, there is often nothing so difficult to understand as a letter. Demetrius (*On Style*, 223) quotes a saying of Artemon, who edited the letters of Aristotle. Artemon said that a letter ought to be written in the same manner as a dialogue, because it was one of the two sides of a discussion. In other words, reading a letter is like listening to one side of a telephone conversation. So, when we read the letters of

Paul, we often find ourselves in difficulty. We do not possess
the letter which he was answering, we do not fully know
the circumstances with which he was dealing, and it is only
from the letter itself that we can deduce the situation which
prompted it. Before we can hope to understand fully any letter
Paul wrote, we must try to reconstruct the situation that
produced it.

The Ancient Letters

It is a great pity that Paul's letters were ever called *epistles*.
They are in the most literal sense *letters*. One of the great
lights shed on the interpretation of the New Testament has
been the discovery and the publication of the *papyri*. In the
ancient world, *papyrus* was the substance on which most
documents were written. It was composed of strips of the
pith of a certain bulrush that grew on the banks of the Nile.
These strips were laid one on top of the other to form a substance very like brown paper. The sands of the Egyptian desert
were ideal for preservation; for papyrus, although very brittle,
will last forever as long as moisture does not get at it. As a
result, from the Egyptian rubbish heaps, archaeologists have
rescued hundreds of documents – marriage contracts, legal
agreements, government forms and, most interesting of all,
private letters. When we read these private letters, we find
that there was a pattern to which nearly all conformed, and
we find that Paul's letters reproduce exactly that pattern. Here
is one of these ancient letters. It is from a soldier, called
Apion, to his father Epimachus. He is writing from Misenum
to tell his father that he has arrived safely after a stormy
passage.

> Apion sends heartiest greetings to his father and lord
> Epimachus. I pray above all that you are well and fit;
> and that things are going well with you and my sister

and her daughter and my brother. I thank my Lord Serapis [his god] that he kept me safe when I was in peril on the sea. As soon as I got to Misenum I got my journey money from Caesar – three gold pieces. And things are going fine with me. So I beg you, my dear father, send me a line, first to let me know how you are, and then about my brothers, and thirdly, that I may kiss your hand, because you brought me up well, and because of that I hope, God willing, soon to be promoted. Give Capito my heartiest greetings, and my brothers and Serenilla and my friends. I sent you a little picture of myself painted by Euctemon. My military name is Antonius Maximus. I pray for your good health. Serenus sends good wishes, Agathos Daimon's boy, and Turbo, Gallonius's son. (G. Milligan, *Selections from the Greek Papyri*, 36)

Little did Apion think that we would be reading his letter to his father some 2,000 years after he had written it. It shows how little human nature changes. The young man is hoping for promotion quickly. Who will Serenilla be but the girl he left behind? He sends the ancient equivalent of a photograph to the family and friends at home. Now, that letter falls into certain sections. (1) There is a greeting. (2) There is a prayer for the health of the recipients. (3) There is a thanksgiving to the gods. (4) There are the special contents. (5) Finally, there are the special salutations and the personal greetings. Practically every one of Paul's letters shows exactly the same sections, as we now demonstrate.

(1) *The greeting*: Romans 1:1; 1 Corinthians 1:1; 2 Corinthians 1:1; Galatians 1:1; Ephesians 1:1; Philippians 1:1; Colossians 1:1–2; 1 Thessalonians 1:1; 2 Thessalonians 1:1.

(2) *The prayer*: in every case, Paul prays for the grace of God on the people to whom he writes: Romans 1:7; 1 Corinthians 1:3; 2 Corinthians 1:2; Galatians 1:3; Ephesians

1:2; Philippians 1:3; Colossians 1:2; 1 Thessalonians 1:1; 2 Thessalonians 1:2.

(3) *The thanksgiving*: Romans 1:8; 1 Corinthians 1:4; 2 Corinthians 1:3; Ephesians 1:3; Philippians 1:3; 1 Thessalonians 1:3; 2 Thessalonians 1:3.

(4) *The special contents*: the main body of the letters.

(5) *The special salutations and personal greetings*: Romans 16; 1 Corinthians 16:19; 2 Corinthians 13:13; Philippians 4:21–2; Colossians 4:12–15; 1 Thessalonians 5:26.

When Paul wrote letters, he wrote them on the pattern which everyone used. The German theologian Adolf Deissmann says of them: 'They differ from the messages of the homely papyrus leaves of Egypt, not as letters but only as the letters of Paul.' When we read Paul's letters, we are reading things which were meant to be not academic exercises and theological treatises, but human documents written by a friend to his friends.

The Immediate Situation

With a very few exceptions, Paul's letters were written to meet an immediate situation. They were not systematic arguments which he sat down to write in the peace and silence of his study. There was some threatening situation in Corinth, or Galatia, or Philippi, or Thessalonica, and he wrote a letter to meet it. He was not in the least thinking of us when he wrote, but solely of the people to whom he was writing. Deissmann writes: 'Paul had no thought of adding a few fresh compositions to the already extant Jewish epistles; still less of enriching the sacred literature of his nation . . . He had no presentiment of the place his words would occupy in universal history; not so much that they would be in existence in the next generation, far less that one day people would look at them as Holy Scripture.' We must always remember that a thing need not be of only passing interest because it was written to meet an immediate situation. Every one of the great love songs of the world was written at a particular time for one person; but they live on for the benefit and enjoyment of all. It is precisely because Paul's letters were written to meet a threatening danger or a pressing need that they still throb with life. And it is because human need and the human situation do not change that God speaks to us through them today.

The Spoken Word

There is one other thing that we must note about these letters. Paul did what most people did in his day. He did not normally pen his own letters, but dictated them to a secretary and then added his own authenticating signature. (We actually know the name of one of the people who did the writing for him. In Romans 16:22, Tertius, the secretary, slips in his own greeting before the letter draws to an end.) In 1 Corinthians 16:21, Paul says in effect: 'This is my own signature, my autograph, so that you can be sure this letter comes from me' (cf. Colossians 4:18; 2 Thessalonians 3:17).

This explains a great deal. Sometimes Paul is hard to understand, because his sentences begin and never finish; his grammar breaks down and the construction becomes complicated. We must not think of him sitting quietly at a desk, carefully polishing each sentence as he writes. We must think of him striding up and down some little room, pouring out a torrent of words, while his secretary races to get them down. When Paul composed his letters, he had in his mind's eye a vision of the people to whom he was writing, and he was pouring out his heart to them in words that fell over each other in his eagerness to help.

The Letter to the Galatians

INTRODUCTION TO THE
LETTER TO THE GALATIANS

Paul under Attack

The letter to the Galatians has been likened to a sword flashing in a great warrior's hand. Both Paul and his gospel were under attack. If that attack had succeeded, Christianity might have become just another Jewish sect, dependent upon circumcision and on keeping the law, instead of being a thing of grace. It is strange to think that, if Paul's opponents had had their way, the gospel might have been kept for Jews and we might never have had the chance to know the love of Christ.

Paul's Apostleship Attacked

It is impossible to possess a vivid personality and a strong character as Paul did and not to encounter opposition; and it is equally impossible to lead such a revolution in religious thought as Paul did and not to be attacked. The first attack was on his apostleship. There were many who said that he was not an apostle at all.

From their own point of view, they were right. In Acts 1:21–2, we have the basic definition of an apostle. Judas the traitor had committed suicide; it was necessary to fill the gap made in the apostolic band. The one to be chosen is described as someone who must be 'one of the men who have accompanied us throughout the time that the Lord Jesus went in

3

and out among us, beginning from the baptism of John until the day when he was taken up from us' and 'a witness with us to his resurrection'. To be an apostle, it was necessary to have kept company with Jesus during his earthly life and to have witnessed his resurrection. That qualification Paul obviously did not fulfil. Further, not so very long ago, he had been the chief persecutor of the Christian Church.

In the very first verse of the letter, Paul answers that challenge. Proudly, he insists that his apostleship is from no human source and that no human hand ordained him to that office, but that he received his call direct from God. Others might have the qualifications demanded when the first vacancy in the apostolic band was filled; but he had a unique qualification – he had met Christ face to face on the Damascus road.

Independence and Agreement

Further, Paul insists that for his message he was dependent on no one. That is why in chapters 1–2 he carefully details his visits to Jerusalem. He is insisting that he is not preaching some second-hand message which he received from a human source; he is preaching a message which he received direct from Christ. But Paul was no anarchist. He insisted that, although the message he received came to him in a unique and personal way, it had received the full approval of those who were the acknowledged leaders of the Christian Church (2:6–10). The gospel he preached came direct from God to him; but it was a gospel in full agreement with the faith delivered to the Church.

The Judaizers

But that gospel was under attack as well. It was a struggle which had to come and a battle which had to be fought. There

4

were Jews who had accepted Christianity; *but* they believed that all God's promises and gifts were for Jews alone and that no Gentile could be admitted to these precious privileges. They therefore believed that Christianity was for Jews and Jews alone. If Christianity was God's greatest gift to men and women, that was all the more reason that only Jews should be allowed to enjoy it. In a way, that was inevitable. There were some Jews who arrogantly believed in the idea of the chosen people. They could say the most terrible things: 'God loves only Israel of all the nations he has made.' 'God will judge Israel with one measure and the Gentiles with another.' 'The best of the snakes crush; the best of the Gentiles kill.' 'God created the Gentiles to be fuel for the fires of Hell.' This was the spirit which made the law lay it down that it was illegal to help a Gentile mother in giving birth, for that would only be to bring another Gentile into the world. When these particular Jews saw Paul bringing the gospel to the despised Gentiles, they were appalled and infuriated.

The Law

There was a way out of this. If Gentiles wanted to become Christians, *let them become Jews first*. What did that mean? It meant that they must be circumcised and take on the whole burden of the law. That, for Paul, was the opposite of all that Christianity meant. It meant that a person's salvation was dependent on the ability to keep the law and could be won by an individual's unaided efforts, whereas, to Paul, salvation was entirely a thing of *grace*. He believed that no one could ever earn the favour of God. All that anyone could do was accept the love God offered by making an act of faith and appealing to God's mercy. A Jew would go to God saying: 'Look! Here is my circumcision. Here are my good deeds.

Give me the salvation I have earned.' Paul would say, as A. M. Toplady's great hymn 'Rock of Ages' expresses it so well:

> Not the labours of my hands
> Can fulfil thy law's demands;
> Could my zeal no respite know,
> Could my tears for ever flow,
> All for sin could not atone:
> Thou must save, and thou alone.
>
> Nothing in my hand I bring,
> Simply to thy cross I cling;
> Naked, come to thee for dress;
> Helpless, look to thee for grace;
> Foul, I to the fountain fly;
> Wash me, Saviour, or I die.

For him, the essential point was not what we could do for God, but what God had done for us.

'But', the Jews argued, 'the greatest thing in our national life is the law. God gave that law to Moses, and on it our very lives depend.' Paul replied: 'Wait a moment. Who is the founder of our nation? To whom were the greatest of God's promises given?' Of course, the answer is Abraham. 'Now,' Paul continued, 'how was it that Abraham gained the favour of God? He could not have gained it by keeping the law, because he lived 430 years before the law was given to Moses. *He gained it by an act of faith.* When God told him to leave his people and go out, Abraham made a sublime act of faith and went, trusting everything to him. It was faith that saved Abraham, not law; and,' Paul goes on, 'it is faith that must save every individual, not deeds of the law. The real child of Abraham is not someone racially descended from him but one who, irrespective of race, makes the same surrender of faith to God.'

The Law and Grace

If all this is true, one very serious question arises: what is the place of the law? It cannot be denied that it was given by God; does this emphasis on grace simply wipe it out?

The law has its own place in the scheme of things. First, it tells us what sin is. If there is no law, we cannot break it and there can be no such thing as sin. Second, and most important, the law really drives us to the grace of God. The trouble about the law is that, because we are all sinful, we can never keep it perfectly. Its effect, therefore, is to show us our weakness and to drive us to a despair in which we see that there is nothing left but to throw ourselves on the mercy and the love of God. The law convinces us of our own insufficiency and in the end compels us to admit that the only thing that can save us is the grace of God. In other words, the law is an essential stage on the way to that grace.

In this epistle, Paul's great theme is the glory of the grace of God and the necessity of realizing that we can never save ourselves.

GALATIANS

THE TRUMPET-CALL OF THE GOSPEL

Galatians 1:1–5

> I, Paul, an apostle – and my apostleship was given to
> me from no human source and through no man's hand,
> because it came to me direct from Jesus Christ and
> from God the Father, who raised Jesus from the dead –
> with all the brothers who are here, write this letter to
> the churches of Galatia. May grace and peace be on
> you from God the Father and from our Lord Jesus
> Christ, who, because our God and Father willed it so,
> gave his life for our sins, to rescue us from this present
> world with all its evil. Glory be to him forever and ever.
> Amen.

To the church of Galatia, some people had come who said
that Paul was not really an apostle and that they need not
listen to what he had to say. They based this attempt to belittle
Paul on the fact that he had not been one of the original
Twelve; that, in fact, he had been the most savage of all
persecutors of the Church, and that he held, as it were, no
official appointment from the leaders of the Church. Paul's
answer was not an argument; it was a statement. He owed his
apostleship not to any human appointment but to a day on
the Damascus road when he had met Jesus Christ face to

face. His authority and his task had been given to him direct from God.

(1) Paul was certain that God had spoken to him. The broadcaster and counsellor Leslie Weatherhead tells of a boy who decided to become a minister. He was asked when he had come to that decision, and he replied that it was after hearing a certain sermon in his school chapel. He was asked the name of the preacher who had brought about such an effect on him. His answer was: 'I do not know the preacher's name; but I know that God spoke to me that day.'

In the last analysis, no one can make another person a minister or a servant of God. Only God himself can do that. The real test of Christians is not whether or not they have gone through certain ceremonies and taken certain vows; it is: have they seen Christ face to face? An old Jewish priest called Ebed-Tob said of the office which he held: 'It was not my father or my mother who installed me in this place, but the arm of the Mighty King gave it to me.'

(2) The real reason for Paul's ability to toil and to suffer was that he was certain his task had been given to him by God. He regarded every effort demanded from him as a God-given task.

It is not only people like Paul who have a task from God; to each one of us God gives a task. It may be one about which everyone will know and which history will remember, or it may be one about which no one will ever hear; but in either case it is a task for God. The great Indian poet and philosopher Tagore has a poem, 'The Gardener', which goes like this:

At midnight the would-be ascetic announced:
　'This is the time to give up my home and seek for God.
　　Ah, who has held me so long in delusion here?'
　God whispered, 'I,' but the ears of the man were stopped.

With a baby asleep at her breast lay his wife, peacefully
     sleeping on one side of the bed.
The man said, 'Who are ye that have fooled me so long?'
The voice said again, 'They are God,' but he heard it not.
The baby cried out in its dream, nestling close to its
     mother.
God commanded, 'Stop, fool, leave not thy home,' but
     still he heard not.
God sighed and complained, 'Why does my servant
     wander to seek me, forsaking me?'

Many humble tasks are a divine commission. As Robert Burns
had it in the 'Epistle to Dr Blacklock',

> To mak' a happy fireside clime
>   For weans and wife,
> That's the true pathos and sublime
>   O' human life.

Paul's God-given task was to evangelize a world; to most of
us, it will simply be to make one or two people happy in the
little circle of those most dear to us.

At the very beginning of his letter, Paul sums up his wishes
and prayers for his friends in two tremendous words.

(1) He wishes them *grace*. There are two main ideas in
this word. The first is that of *sheer beauty*. The Greek word
charis means grace in the theological sense; but it always
means beauty and charm; and, even when used in a theological sense, the idea of charm is never far away from it. If
the Christian life has grace in it, it must be a lovely thing. Far
too often, goodness exists without charm and charm without
goodness. It is when goodness and charm unite that the work
of grace is seen. The second idea is that of *undeserved
generosity*, of a gift, which is never deserved and could never
be earned, given in the generous love of God. When Paul

prays for grace to be bestowed on his friends, it is as if he were saying: 'May the beauty of the undeserved love of God be on you, so that it will make your life lovely, too.'

(2) He wishes them *peace*. Paul was a Jew, and the Jewish word *shalom* must have been in his mind, even as he wrote the Greek word *eirene*. *Shalom* means far more than the mere absence of trouble. It means everything which is to our highest good, everything which will make the mind pure, the will resolute and the heart glad. It is that sense of the love and care of God, which, even if our bodies are tortured, can keep our hearts serene.

Finally, Paul sums up in one sentence of infinite meaning the heart and the work of Jesus Christ. 'He gave himself . . . to rescue us.' (1) The love of Christ is a love *which gave and suffered*. (2) The love of Christ is a love *which conquered and achieved*. In this life, the tragedy of love is that it is so often frustrated; but the love of Christ is backed by an infinite power which nothing can frustrate and which can rescue its loved one from the bondage of sin.

THE SLAVE OF CHRIST

Galatians 1:6–10

> I am amazed that you have so quickly deserted him who called you by the grace of Christ, and that you have so soon gone over to a different gospel, a gospel which in point of fact is not another gospel at all. What has really happened is that certain men are upsetting your whole faith and are aiming at reversing the gospel of Christ. But even if we or an angel from heaven were to preach a gospel to you, other than that which you have received, let him be accursed. Is it men's favour I am trying to win, or is it God's? Or am I

seeking to curry favour with men? If after all that has
happened to me I were still trying to curry favour with
men, I would not be bearing the brands of the slave of
Christ.

THE basic fact behind this letter is that Paul's gospel was a
gospel of free grace. He believed with all his heart that
nothing anyone could do could ever earn the love of God,
and that therefore all that people could do was fling themselves on God's mercy in an act of faith. All they could do
was take in wondering gratitude what God offered; the
important thing was not what we could do for ourselves but
what God had done for us.

It was this gospel of the free grace of God that Paul had
preached. After him, there came others preaching a Jewish
version of Christianity. They declared that, if people wanted
to please God, they must be circumcised and then dedicate
their lives to carrying out all the rules and regulations of the
law. Every time a deed of the law was performed, so they
said, that was a credit entry in a person's account with God.
They were teaching that it was necessary to earn the favour
of God. To Paul, that was utterly impossible.

Paul's opponents declared that he was making religion
far too easy and was doing so to ingratiate himself with
others. In fact, that accusation was the reverse of the truth.
After all, if religion consists in fulfilling a set of rules and
regulations, it is, at least theoretically, possible to satisfy
its demands; but Paul is holding up the cross and saying:
'God loved you like that.' Religion becomes a matter not
of satisfying the claims of *law* but of trying to meet the
obligation of *love*. We can satisfy the claims of law, for they
have strict and statutory limits; but we can never satisfy the
claims of love, for, if we gave our loved ones the sun, the

moon and the stars, we still would be left feeling that that was an offering far too small. But all that Paul's Jewish opponents could see was that he had declared that circumcision was no longer necessary and the law no longer relevant.

Paul denied that he was trying to ingratiate himself with others. It was not other people he was serving; it was God. It made no difference to him what people said or thought about him; his master was God. And then he brought forward an unanswerable argument: 'If I were trying to gain favour with other people, I would not be the slave of Christ.' What is in his mind is this: slaves had their master's name and sign stamped on them with a red-hot branding iron; Paul himself bore on his body the marks of his sufferings, the brand of the slavery of Christ. 'If,' he said, 'I were out to gain favour with other people, would I have these scars on my body?' The fact that he was marked in this way was the final proof that his aim was to serve Christ and not to please others.

The American author and journalist John Gunther tells us of the very early communists in Russia. Many of them had been in prison under the Tsarist regime and bore on their bodies the physical marks of what they had suffered; and he tells us that, far from being ashamed of the marks which disfigured them, these were their greatest pride. We might think that they were misguided and misguiding, but we cannot doubt the genuineness of their allegiance to the communist cause.

It is when people see that we are prepared to suffer for the faith which we say we hold that they begin to believe that we really hold it. If our faith costs us nothing, others will value it at nothing.

THE HAND OF GOD INTERVENES

Galatians 1:11-17

> As for the gospel that has been preached by me, I want
> you to know, brothers, that it rests on no human
> foundation, for neither did I receive it from any man,
> nor was I taught it, but it came to me through direct
> revelation from Jesus Christ. If you want proof of that,
> you heard of the kind of life I once lived when I
> practised the Jewish faith, a life in which I persecuted
> the Church of God beyond all bounds and devastated it.
> I was making strides in the Jewish faith beyond many
> of my contemporaries in my nation, for I was zealous
> to excess for the traditions of my fathers. It was then
> that God, who had set me apart for a special task before
> I was born, and who called me through his grace,
> decided to reveal his Son through me, that I might tell
> the good news of him among the Gentiles. Thereupon I
> did not confer with any human being, nor did I go up to
> Jerusalem to see those who were apostles before I was;
> but I went away to Arabia; and then I went back again
> to Damascus.

IT was Paul's contention that the gospel he preached was not
simply something he had heard from others; it had come to
him direct from God. That was a bold claim to make, and it
demanded some kind of proof. For that proof, Paul had the
courage to point to himself and to the radical change in his
own life.

(1) *He had been a fanatic for the law*; and now the
dominant centre of his life was *grace*. This man, who had
with passionate intensity tried to *earn* God's favour, was now
content in humble faith to take what God lovingly offered.
He had ceased to glory in what he could do for himself, and
had begun to glory in what God had done for him.

(2) *He had been the chief persecutor of the Church.* He
had 'devastated' the Church. The word he uses is the word
for utterly destroying a city. He had tried to make a scorched
earth of the Church; and now his one aim, which he was
prepared to devote himself to and even to die for, was to
spread that same Church over all the world.

By the laws of cause and effect, everything that happens
must have an adequate cause. When someone is proceeding
headlong in one direction and suddenly turns and proceeds
headlong in the opposite direction; when quite suddenly all
values are reversed so that that person's life turns upside
down, some explanation is required. For Paul, the explanation
was the direct intervention of God. He had laid his hand on
his shoulder and stopped him in mid-career. 'That', said Paul,
'is the kind of effect which only God could produce.' It is a
notable thing about Paul that he is not afraid to recount the
record of his own shame in order to show God's power.

He has two things to say about that intervention.

(1) It was not unpremeditated; it was in God's eternal plan.
A. J. Gossip, Professor at Trinity College, Glasgow, tells
how Alexander Whyte, the great preacher and Principal of
New College, Edinburgh, preached the sermon when he was
ordained to his first charge. Whyte's message was that, all
through time and eternity, God had been preparing this man
for this congregation and this congregation for this man and,
on time to the minute, he had brought them together.

God sends every individual into the world with a part to
play in his purpose. It may be a big part or it may be a small
part. It may be to do something of which the whole world
will know or something of which only a few will ever know.
The Stoic philosopher Epictetus (*Discourses* 2:16) says:
'Have courage to look up to God and to say, "Deal with me
as you will from now on. I am as one with you; I am yours; I

flinch from nothing as long as you think that it is good. Lead me where you will; put on me what raiment you will. Would you have me hold office, or reject it, stay or fly, be rich or poor? For all this I will defend you before men." ' If a philosopher from Ancient Greece could give himself so wholly to a God whom he knew so dimly, how much more should we!

(2) Paul knew himself to be chosen for a task. He thought of himself as chosen not for honour but for service, not for an easy life but for battles. It is for the hardest campaigns that generals choose their best soldiers and for the hardest studies that teachers choose their best students. Paul knew that he had been saved to serve.

THE WAY OF THE CHOSEN

Galatians 1:18-25

> Then, three years after that, I went up to Jerusalem to visit Cephas, and I stayed with him a fortnight. I saw no other apostle except James, the Lord's brother. As for what I am writing to you – before God I am not lying. Then I went to the districts of Syria and Cilicia. But I remained personally unknown to the churches of Judaea which are in Christ. The only thing they knew about me was that they were hearing the news – our one-time persecutor is preaching the faith which once he tried to devastate – and they found in me cause to glorify God.

WHEN we look at this passage alongside the last section of the preceding one, we see just what Paul did when the hand of God stopped him in his tracks.

(1) First, he went away to *Arabia*. He went away to be alone, and for two reasons. First, he had to think out this

tremendous thing that had happened to him. Second, he had to speak with God before he spoke to other people.

There are so few who will take the time to face themselves and to face God; and how can anyone meet the temptations, stresses and strains of life without first thinking things out and thinking them through?

(2) Second, he went back to *Damascus*. That was a courageous thing to do. He had been on the way to Damascus to wipe out the Church when God intervened – and all Damascus knew that. He went back at once to bear his testimony to the people who knew best what he had been.

Rudyard Kipling has a famous poem called 'Mulholland's Vow'. Mulholland was a cattleman on a ship. A storm broke out, and in the storm the cattle broke loose. Mulholland made a bargain with God that, if he saved him from the plunging horns and hooves, he would serve him from that time on. When he got safely to land, he proposed to keep his part of the bargain; but his idea was to preach religion where no one knew him. Then came God's command: 'Back you go to the cattle-boats and preach my gospel *there*.' God sent him back to the place that he knew and that knew him. Our Christian witness, like our Christian charity, must begin at home.

(3) Third, Paul went to *Jerusalem*. Again he took his life in his hands. His former friends, the Jews, would be out for his blood, because to them he was a deserter. His former victims, the Christians, might well ostracize him, unable to believe that he was a changed man.

Paul had the courage to face his past. We never really get away from our past by running away from it. We can deal with it only by facing it and defeating it.

(4) Fourth, Paul went to *Syria and Cilicia*. That was where Tarsus was. It was there that he had been brought up. There were the friends of his boyhood and his youth. Again he chose

the hard way. They would no doubt regard him as quite mad; they would meet him with anger, and, worse, with mockery. But he was quite prepared to be regarded as a fool for the sake of Christ.

In these verses, Paul was seeking to defend and prove the independence of his gospel. He got it from no human source; he got it from God. He consulted no one else; he consulted God. But, as he wrote, he unconsciously presented himself as the man who had the courage to witness to his change and preach his gospel in the hardest places of all.

THE MAN WHO REFUSED TO BE INTIMIDATED

Galatians 2:1-10

> Fourteen years afterwards I again went up to Jerusalem with Barnabas, and I took Titus with me too. It was in consequence of a direct message from God that I went up; and I placed before them the gospel that I am accustomed to preach among the Gentiles, because I did not want to think that the work which I was trying to do, and which I had done, was going to be frustrated. This I did in private conference with those whose reputations stood high in the Church. But not even Titus, who was with me, was compelled to be circumcised, although he was a Greek. True, they tried to circumcise him to please false brothers who had been furtively introduced into our society and who had insinuated themselves into our company to spy out the liberty which we enjoy in Christ Jesus, because they wished to reduce us to their own state of servitude. Not for one hour did we yield in submission to them. We took a stand that the truth of the gospel might remain with you. Now, from those who are men of reputation – what they once were makes

no difference to me – there is no favouritism with God – those men of reputation imparted no fresh knowledge to me; but, on the other hand, when they saw that I had been entrusted with the preaching of the gospel in the non-Jewish world, just as Peter had been in the Jewish world – for he who worked for Peter, to make him the apostle of the Jewish world, worked for me too to make me the apostle to the non-Jewish world – and when they realized the grace that had been given to me, James, Cephas and John, whom all look upon as pillars of the Church, gave pledges of partnership to me and to Barnabas, in complete agreement that we should go to the non-Jewish world, and they to the Jewish world. The one thing which they did enjoin us to do was to remember the poor – the very thing that I myself was eager to do.

In the preceding passage, Paul has proved the independence of his gospel; here, he is concerned to prove that this independence is not anarchy and that his gospel is not something divisive and sectarian, but nothing less than the faith delivered to the Church.

After fourteen years' work, he went up to Jerusalem, taking with him Titus, a young friend and supporter, who was a Greek. That visit was by no means easy. Even as he wrote, Paul was clearly agitated. There is a confusion in the Greek which it is not possible fully to reproduce in English translation. Paul's problem was that he could not say too little, or he might seem to be abandoning his principles; and he could not say too much, or it might seem that he was openly at variance with the leaders of the Church. The result was that his sentences are broken and disjointed, reflecting his anxiety.

From the beginning, the real leaders of the Church accepted his position; but there were others who were out to tame this fiery spirit. There were those who, as we have seen, accepted Christianity but believed that God never gave any privilege to anyone who was not a Jew, and that therefore, before a man could become a Christian, he must be circumcised and take the whole law upon him. These Judaizers, as they are called, seized on Titus as a test case. There is a battle behind this passage; and it seems likely that the leaders of the Church urged Paul, for the sake of peace, to give in, in the case of Titus. But Paul stood firm like a rock. He knew that to give in would be to accept the slavery of the law and to turn his back on the freedom which is in Christ. In the end, Paul's determination won the day. In principle, it was accepted that his work lay in the non-Jewish world, and the work of Peter and James among the Jews. It should be carefully noted that it is not a question of two different gospels being preached; it is a question of the same gospel being brought to two different spheres by different people specially qualified to do so.

From this picture, certain characteristics of Paul emerge clearly.

(1) He was a man who gave authority its due respect. He did not go his own way. He went and talked with the leaders of the Church, however much he might differ from them. It is a great and neglected law of life that, however right we happen to be, there is nothing to be gained by rudeness. There is never any reason why courtesy and determination should not go hand in hand.

(2) He was a man who refused to be intimidated. Repeatedly, he mentions the reputation which the leaders and pillars of the Church enjoyed. He respected them and treated them with courtesy; but he remained inflexible. There is such a thing as respect; and there is such a thing as grovelling and bowing to those whom the world or the Church labels great,

simply because it is expected. Paul was always certain that he was seeking the approval not of the world but of God.

(3) He was a man conscious of a special task. He was convinced that God had given him a task to do, and he would let neither opposition from without nor discouragement from within stop him doing it. Those who know they have a God-given task will always find that they have a God-given strength to carry it out.

THE ESSENTIAL UNITY

Galatians 2:11-13

> But when Peter came to Antioch, I opposed him to his face because he stood condemned. Before some men arrived from James, it was his habit to eat with the Gentiles. When they came, he withdrew and separated himself, because he was scared of the circumcision party. The rest of the Jews played the hypocrite along with him, so that even Barnabas was led away along with them by their hypocritical actions.

THE trouble was by no means at an end. Part of the life of the early Church was a common meal which they called the *Agape* or Love Feast. At this feast, the whole congregation came together to enjoy a common meal provided by pooling whatever resources they had. For many of the slaves, it must have been the only decent meal they had all week; and in a very special way, it marked the togetherness of the Christians.

That seems, on the face of it, a lovely thing. But we must remember the rigid exclusiveness of the more narrow-minded Jews who regarded their race as the chosen people in such a way as involved the rejection of all others. 'The Lord is merciful and gracious' (Exodus 34:6; Psalm 103:8). 'But he

is only gracious to Israelites; other nations he will terrify.'
'The nations are as stubble or straw which shall be burned,
or as chaff scattered to the wind.' 'If a man repents, God
accepts him, but that applies only to Israel and no other
nation.' 'Love all but hate the heretics.' This exclusiveness
affected daily life. Strict Jews were forbidden even to do
business with Gentiles; they must not go on a journey with
Gentiles; they must neither give hospitality to, nor accept
hospitality from, Gentiles.

Here in Antioch, a tremendous problem arose – in this
situation, could the Jews and the Gentiles sit down together
at a common meal? If the old law was to be observed, it was
obviously impossible. Peter came to Antioch and, at first,
disregarding the old taboos in the glory of the new faith, he
shared the common meal with both Jews and Gentiles. Then
some members of the Jewish party from Jerusalem arrived.
They used James' name, although quite certainly they were
not representing his views, and they worked on Peter so much
that he withdrew from the common meal. The other Jews
withdrew with him, and finally even Barnabas was involved
in this withdrawal. It was then that Paul spoke with all the
intensity of which his passionate nature was capable, for he
saw certain things quite clearly.

(1) A church ceases to be Christian if it contains class
distinctions. In the presence of God, people are neither Jews
nor Gentiles, noble nor of low birth, rich nor poor; they are
all sinners for whom Christ died. If we are all children of
God, we must be one family.

(2) Paul saw that forceful action was necessary to
counteract a drift which had occurred. He did not wait; he
struck. It made no difference to him that this drifting was
connected with the name and conduct of Peter. It was wrong,
and that was all that mattered to him. A famous name can

never justify an infamous action. Paul's action gives us a vivid example of how one strong individual by determination can halt a drift away from the right course before it becomes a tidal wave.

THE END OF THE LAW

Galatians 2:14–17

> But when I saw that they were straying away from the right path which the gospel lays down, I said to Peter in front of them all: 'If you who are a born Jew choose to live like a Gentile and not like a Jew, why are you forcing the Gentiles to live like Jews? We are by nature Jews; we are not Gentile sinners as you would call them; and we know that a man is not put right with God because he does the works which the law lays down, but through faith in Jesus Christ. Now, we have accepted this faith in Jesus Christ, so that we might be right with God, and that faith has nothing to do with the works the law lays down, because no man can ever put himself right with God by doing the works the law lays down. Now, if in our search to be made right with God through Christ Jesus we too become what you call sinners, are you then going to argue that Christ is the minister of sin? God forbid!'

HERE at last, the real root of the matter is being reached. A decision is being forced which could not in any event be long delayed. The fact of the matter was that the Jerusalem decision was a compromise, and, like all compromises, it had in it the seeds of trouble. In effect, the decision was that the Jews would go on living like Jews, observing circumcision and the law, but that the Gentiles were free from these observances. Clearly, things could not go on like that, because the inevitable result was that there were now two grades of Christians and two quite distinct classes in the Church. Paul's argument ran like this. He said to Peter: 'You shared a table with the Gentiles; you ate as they ate; therefore you approved in principle that there is one way for Jews and Gentiles alike. How can you now reverse your decision and want the Gentiles to be circumcised and take the law upon them?' It did not make sense to Paul.

Now, we must make sure of the meaning of one word. When the Jews used the word *sinners* of Gentiles, they were not thinking of moral qualities; they were thinking of the actions that broke the law. To take an example, Leviticus 11 lays down which animals may and may not be used for food. Someone who ate a hare or pork broke these laws and became a *sinner* in this sense of the term. On that basis, Peter's response to Paul would be: 'But, if I eat with the Gentiles and eat the things they eat, I become a sinner.'

Paul's answer was twofold. First, he said: 'We agreed long ago that no amount of observance of the law can make a person right with God. That is a matter of grace. We cannot earn, but must accept the generous offer of the love of God in Jesus. Therefore the whole business of law is irrelevant.' Next, he said: 'You hold that to forget all this business about rules and regulations will make you a sinner. *But that is precisely what Jesus Christ told you to do*. He did not tell you to try to earn salvation by eating this animal and not eating that one. He told you to fling yourself without reserve on the grace of God. Are you going to argue, then, that he taught you to become a sinner?' Obviously, there could be only one proper conclusion, namely that the old laws were wiped out.

This is the point that had to come. It could not be right for Gentiles to come to God by grace and for Jews to come to God by law. For Paul, there was only one reality – grace –

and it was by way of surrender to that grace that all must come.

There are two great temptations in the Christian life; and, in a certain sense, the better people are, the more susceptible they are to them. First, there is the temptation to try to earn God's favour, and second, the temptation to use some little achievement to compare oneself with others to our advantage and their disadvantage. But the Christianity which has enough of self left in it to think that by its own efforts it can please God and that by its own achievements it can show itself superior to others is not true Christianity at all.

THE LIFE THAT IS CRUCIFIED AND RISEN

Galatians 2:18–21

> If I build up again these very things that I destroyed, I simply succeed in making myself a transgressor. For through the law I died to the law that I might live to God. I have been crucified with Christ. True, I am alive; but it is no longer I who live but Christ who lives in me. The life that I am now living, although it is still in the flesh, is a life which is lived in faith in the Son of God, who loved me and gave himself for me. I am not going to cancel out the grace of God; for, if I can get right with God by means of the law, then Christ died quite unnecessarily.

PAUL speaks out of the depths of personal experience. For him to put back in place the whole fabric of the law would have been spiritual suicide. He says that through the law he died to the law that he might live to God. What he means is this: he had tried the way of law; he had tried with all the terrible intensity of his burning conviction to put himself right with God by a life that sought to obey every single item of that law. He had found that such an attempt produced nothing but a deeper and deeper sense that all he could do could never put him right with God. All the law had done was to show him his own helplessness. Thereupon, he had quite suddenly abandoned that way and had cast himself, sinner as he was, on the mercy of God. It was the law which had driven him to God. To go back to the law would simply have entangled him all over again in the sense of estrangement from God. So great was the change that the only way he could describe it was to say that he had been crucified with Christ so that the man he used to be was dead and the living power within him now was Christ himself.

'If I can put myself to rights with God by meticulously obeying the law, then what is the need of grace? If I can win my own salvation, then why did Christ have to die?' Paul was quite sure of one thing – that Jesus Christ had done for him what he could never have done for himself. The one man who re-enacted the experience of Paul was the great reformer Martin Luther. Luther was a model of discipline and penance, self-denial and self-torture. 'If ever', he said, 'a man could be saved by being a monk, that man was I.' He had gone to Rome; it was considered to be an act of great merit to climb the Scala Sancta, the great sacred stairway, on hands and knees. He toiled upwards seeking that merit, and suddenly there came to him the voice from heaven: 'The just shall live by faith.' The life at peace with God was not to be attained by this futile, never-ending, ever-defeated effort; it could be achieved only by casting himself on the love and mercy of God as Jesus Christ revealed them to men and women. As the hymn-writer F. W. Faber had it:

Pining souls! come nearer Jesus,
   And O come, not doubting thus,
But with faith that trusts more bravely
   His huge tenderness for us.

If our love were but more simple,
   We should take him at his word;
And our lives would be all sunshine,
   In the sweetness of our Lord.

When Paul took God at his word, the midnight of law's frustration became the sunshine of grace.

THE GIFT OF GRACE

Galatians 3:1–9

O senseless Galatians, who has put the evil eye on you – you before whose very eyes Jesus Christ was placarded upon his cross? Tell me this one thing – did you receive the Spirit by doing the works the law lays down, or because you listened and believed? Are you so senseless? After beginning your experience of God in the Spirit, are you now going to try to complete it by making it dependent upon what human nature can do? Is the tremendous experience you had all for nothing – if indeed you are going to let it go for nothing? Did he who generously gave you the Spirit, and who wrought mighty things among you, do so because you produced the deeds the law lays down, or because you heard and believed? Was it not with you exactly as it was with Abraham? Abraham trusted God, and it was that which was credited to him as righteousness. So you must realize that it is those who make the venture of faith who are the sons of Abraham. Scripture foresaw that it would be by faith that God would bring the Gentiles

into a right relationship with himself, and told the good
news to Abraham before it happened – in you shall all
nations be blessed. So, then, it is those who make that
same venture of faith who are blessed along with
Abraham, the man of faith.

PAUL uses a further argument to show that it is faith and not
works of the law which puts us right with God. In the early
Church, converts nearly always received the Holy Spirit in a
visible way. The early chapters of Acts show this happening
again and again (cf. Acts 8:14–17, 10:44). There came to
them a new surge of life and power that anyone could see.
That experience had happened to the Galatians and had
happened, said Paul, not because they had obeyed the
regulations of the law – because at that time they had never
heard of the law – but because they had heard the good news
of the love of God and had responded to it in an act of perfect
trust.

The easiest way to grasp an idea is to see it embodied in a
person. In a sense, every great word must become flesh. So,
Paul pointed the Galatians to a man who embodied faith –
Abraham. He was the man to whom God had made the great
promise that in him all families of the earth would be blessed
(Genesis 12:3). He was the man whom God had specially
chosen as the one who pleased him. How did Abraham
especially please God? It was not by doing the works of the
law, because at that time the law did not exist; it was by
taking God at his word in a great act of faith.

Now, the promise of blessedness was made to the descendants of Abraham. The Jews relied on that; they held that
simple physical descent from Abraham set them on a different
footing with God from other people. Paul declares that to be
a true descendant of Abraham is not a matter of flesh and

blood; the real descendant is the one who makes the same venture of faith. Therefore, it is not those who seek merit through the law who inherit the promise made to Abraham, but those of every nation who repeat his act of faith in God. It was by an act of faith that the Galatians had begun. Surely they are not going to slip back into legalism – and lose their inheritance?

This passage is full of Greek words with a history, words which carried an atmosphere and a story with them. In verse 1, Paul speaks about *the evil eye*. The Greeks had a great fear of a spell cast by the evil eye. Time and again, private letters end with a sentence such as this: 'Above all I pray that you may be in health *unharmed by the evil eye* and faring prosperously' (G. Milligan, *Selections from the Greek Papyri*, No. 14).

In the same verse, Paul talks about Jesus Christ being *placarded* before them upon his cross. It is the Greek word (*prographein*) that would be used for putting up a poster. It is actually used for a notice put up by a father to say that he will no longer be responsible for his son's debts; it is also used for putting up the announcement of an auction.

In verse 4, Paul talks about *beginning* their experience in the Spirit and *ending* it in the flesh. The words he uses are the normal Greek words for beginning and completing a sacrifice. The first one (*enarchesthai*) is the word for scattering the grains of barley on and around the victim, which was the first act of a sacrifice; and the second one (*epiteleisthai*) is the word used for fully completing the ritual of any sacrifice. By using these two words, Paul shows that he looks on the Christian life as a sacrifice to God.

In verse 5, he speaks of God giving generously to the Galatians. The root of this word is the Greek *choregia*. In ancient times in Greece, at the great festivals, the great dramatists like Euripides and Sophocles presented their plays. Greek plays all have a chorus; to equip and train a chorus was expensive, and public-spirited Greeks generously offered to pay the entire expenses of the chorus. (That gift is described by the word *choregia*.) Later, in wartime, patriotic citizens gave free contributions to the state, and *choregia* was used for this too. In still later Greek, in the papyri, the word is common in marriage contracts and describes the support that a husband, out of his love, undertakes to give his wife. *Choregia* underlines the generosity of God, a generosity which comes from love, of which the love of citizens for their city and of a husband for his wife are pale shadows.

THE CURSE OF THE LAW

Galatians 3:10–14

> All who depend on the deeds which the law lays down are under a curse, for it stands written: 'Cursed is everyone who does not consistently obey and perform all the things written in the book of the law.' It is clear that no one ever gets into a right relationship with God by means of this legalism, because, as the Bible says, 'It is the man who is right with God through faith who will live.' But the law is not based on faith. And yet the Scripture says: 'The man who does these things will have to live by them.' Christ ransomed us from the curse of the law by becoming accursed for us – for it stands written: 'Cursed is every man who is hanged on a tree.' And this all happened so that in Christ Abraham's blessing should come to the Gentiles, and so that we might receive the promised Spirit by means of faith.

PAUL's argument seeks to drive his opponents into a corner from which there is no escape. 'Suppose', he says, 'you decide that you are going to try to win God's approval by accepting and obeying the law, what is the inevitable consequence?' First of all, those who do that have to stand or fall by their decision; if they choose the law, they have to live by it. Second, no one has ever succeeded and no one will ever succeed in always keeping the law. Third, that being so, you are accursed, because Scripture itself says (Deuteronomy 27:26) that anyone who does not keep the whole law is cursed. Therefore, the inevitable result of trying to get right with God by making the law the principle of life is a curse.

But Scripture has another saying: 'It is the one who is right with God by faith who will really live' (cf. Habakkuk 2:4). The only way to get into a right relationship with God, and therefore the only way to peace, is the way of faith. But the principle of law and the principle of faith are direct opposites; you cannot live your life by both at one and the same time; you must choose; and the only logical choice is to abandon the way of legalism and to venture upon the way of faith, of taking God at his word and of trusting in his love.

How can we know that this is so? The final guarantor of its truth is Jesus Christ; and to bring this truth to us he had to die upon a cross. Now, Scripture says that everyone who is hanged on a tree is under God's curse (Deuteronomy 21:23); and so, to free us from the curse of the law, Jesus himself had to become accursed.

Even at his most involved, and here he is involved, one simple yet tremendous fact is never far from the mind and heart of Paul – *the cost of the Christian gospel*. He could never forget that the peace, the liberty, the right relationship with God that we possess, cost the life and death of Jesus Christ – for how could we have ever known what God was like unless Jesus Christ had died to tell us of his great love?

THE COVENANT THAT CANNOT
BE ALTERED

Galatians 3:15–18

> Brothers, I can use only a human analogy. Here is the
> parallel – when a covenant is duly ratified, even if it is
> only a man's covenant, no one annuls it or adds
> additional clauses to it. Now, the promises were made
> to Abraham and to his *seed*. It does not say 'and to his
> *seeds*', as if it were a case of *many*, but 'and to his
> *seed*', as if it were a case of *one*, and that one is Christ.
> This is what I mean: the law which came into being
> 430 years later cannot annul the covenant already
> ratified by God and thus render the promise inoperative.
> For, if the inheritance is dependent on law, it is no longer
> dependent on promise; but it was through promise that
> God conferred his grace on Abraham.

WHEN we read passages like this and the next one, we have to
remember that Paul was a trained Rabbi, an expert in the
scholastic methods of the Rabbinic academies. He could, and
did, use their methods of argument, which would be completely convincing to a Jew, however difficult it may be for
us to understand them.

His aim is to show the superiority of the way of grace
over the way of law. He begins by showing that the way of
grace is older than the way of law. When Abraham made his
venture of faith, God made his great promise to him. That is
to say, God's promise was the result of an act of faith; the
law did not come until the time of Moses, 430 years later.
But – Paul goes on to argue – once a covenant has been duly
ratified, you cannot alter it or add additional clauses to it.
Therefore, the later law cannot alter the earlier way of faith.
It was faith which set Abraham right with God; and faith is

still the only way for men and women to set themselves right with God.

The Rabbis were very fond of using arguments which depended on the interpretation of single words; they would construct a whole theology on one word. Paul takes one word in the Abraham story and builds an argument upon it. As the Authorized Version translates Genesis 17:7–8, God says to Abraham: 'I will establish my covenant between me and thee and thy *seed* after thee', and says of his inheritance: 'I will give it unto thee and to thy *seed* after thee.' (*Seed* is more clearly rendered as *descendant*, as the Revised Standard Version has it.) Paul's argument is that *seed* is used in the *singular* and not in the *plural*, and that, therefore, God's promise points not to a great crowd of people but to *one single individual*; and – Paul argues – the one person in whom the covenant finds its fulfilment is Jesus Christ. Therefore, the way to peace with God is the way of faith which Abraham took; and we must repeat that way by looking to Jesus Christ in faith.

Again and again, Paul comes back to the same point. The problem of human life is to get into a right relationship with God. As long as we are afraid of him, there can be no peace. How are we to achieve this right relationship? Is it by a meticulous and even self-torturing obedience to the law, by performing endless actions and observing every smallest regulation the law lays down? If we take that way, we will always be in default, for human imperfection can never fully satisfy God's perfection; but, if we abandon this hopeless struggle and bring ourselves and our sin to God, his grace opens its arms to us and we find ourselves at peace with a God who is no longer judge but father. Paul's argument is that this is what happened to Abraham. It was on that basis that God's covenant with Abraham was made; and nothing that came in later can change that covenant any more than anything can alter a will that has already been witnessed and signed.

IMPRISONED UNDER SIN

Galatians 3:19–22

> Why, then, have the law at all? The law was added to the situation to define what transgressions are, until the seed should come, to whom the promise, which still holds good, had been made. That law was enacted by angels and came by means of a mediator. Now, there can be no such thing as a mediator of one; and God is one. Is, then, the law contrary to the promises of God? God forbid! If a law which was able to give life had been given, then indeed right relationship with God would have come through the law. But the words of Scripture shut up everything under the power of sin, for the very reason that the promise should be given to those who believe through faith in Jesus Christ.

THIS is one of the most difficult passages Paul ever wrote – so difficult that there are almost 300 different interpretations of it! Let us begin by remembering that Paul is still seeking to demonstrate the superiority of the way of grace and faith over the way of law. He makes four points about the law.

(1) Why introduce the law at all? It was introduced, as Paul puts it, *for the sake of transgressions*. What he means is that where there is no law there is no sin. People cannot be condemned for doing wrong if they did not know that it was wrong. Therefore the function of the law is *to define sin*. But, while the law can and does define sin, it can do nothing whatever to cure it. It is like a doctor who is an expert in

35

diagnosing illness but who is helpless to clear up the trouble which has been diagnosed.

(2) The law was not given direct by God. In the old story in Exodus 20, it *was* given direct to Moses; but, in the days of Paul, the Rabbis were so impressed by the holiness and the remoteness of God that they believed that it was quite impossible for him to deal direct with men and women; therefore they introduced the idea that the law was given first to angels and then by the angels to Moses (cf. Acts 7:53; Hebrews 2:2). Here, Paul is using the Rabbinic ideas of his time. The law is distanced from God by two stages. It is given first to angels, and then to a mediator; and the mediator is Moses. Compared with the *promise*, which was given directly by God, the *law* comes as second-hand.

(3) Now we come to that extraordinarily difficult sentence – 'There can be no such thing as a mediator of one; and God is one.' What is Paul's idea here? An agreement founded on law always involves *two* people – the person who gives it and the person who accepts it – and it depends on both sides keeping it. That was the position of those who put their trust in the law. Break the law, and the whole agreement was undone. But a promise depends on only *one* person. The way of grace depends entirely on God; it is his promise. We can do nothing to alter that. We may sin, but the love and the grace of God stand unchanged. To Paul, it was the weakness of the law that it depended on *two* persons – the law-giver and the law-keeper – and human beings had wrecked it. Grace is entirely from God; we cannot undo it; and surely it is better to depend on the grace of the unchanging God than on the hopeless efforts of helpless human beings.

(4) Is, then, the law opposed to grace? Logically, Paul should answer: 'Yes'; but in fact he answers: 'No.' He says that Scripture has imprisoned everyone under sin. He is

thinking of Deuteronomy 27:26, where it is said that everyone who does not conform to the words of the law is cursed. In fact, that means *everyone*, because no one has ever kept, or will ever perfectly keep, the law. What, then, is the consequence of the law? It is to drive everyone to seek grace, because it has proved human helplessness. This is a thought that Paul will soon develop in the next chapter; here, he only suggests it. Let anyone try to get into a right relationship with God via the law. Those who make the attempt will find they cannot do it and will be driven to see that all they can do is to accept the wonderful grace of which Jesus Christ came to tell all people.

THE COMING OF FAITH

Galatians 3:23-9

> Before faith came, we were under guard under the power of the law, shut up and waiting for the day when faith would be revealed. So, the law was really our tutor to bring us to Christ so that we might get into a right relationship with God by means of faith. But now that faith has come, we are no longer under a tutor; for you are all sons of God through faith in Christ Jesus. As many of you as have been baptized into Christ have put on Christ. There is no longer any distinction between Jew and Greek, slave and free man, male and female, for you are all one in Christ Jesus. And if you belong to Christ, then you are the seed of Abraham, and heirs according to promise.

PAUL is still thinking of the essential part that the law did play in the plan of God. In the Greek world, there was a household servant called the *paidagogos*. He was not the

37

schoolmaster. He was usually an old and trusted slave who had been in the family for a long time and who was well respected. He was in charge of the children's moral welfare, and it was his duty to see that they acquired the qualities essential to mature adulthood. He had one particular duty: every day, he had to take the children to and from school. He had nothing to do with the actual teaching of the children, but it was his duty to take them in safety to the school and deliver them to the teacher. That – said Paul – was like the function of the law. It was there to lead people to Christ. It could not take them into Christ's presence, but it could take them into a position where they might enter for themselves. It was the function of the law to bring men and women to Christ by showing them that by themselves they were quite unable to keep it. But, once people had come to Christ, they no longer needed the law, for now they were dependent not on law but on grace.

'As many of you', says Paul, 'as have been baptized into Christ have put on Christ.' There are two vivid pictures here. Baptism was a Jewish rite. If a man wanted to accept the Jewish faith, he had to do three things. He had to be circumcised, to offer sacrifice and to be baptized. Ceremonial washing to cleanse from defilement was common practice in Judaism (cf. Leviticus 11–15).

The details of Jewish baptism were as follows. The man to be baptized cut his hair and his nails; he undressed completely; the baptismal bath had to contain forty seahs, that is about 280 litres, of water. Every part of the body had to be touched with the water. He made confession of his faith before three men who were called *fathers of baptism*. While he was still in the water, parts of the law were read to him, words of encouragement were addressed to him, and blessings were pronounced upon him. When he emerged, he was a member of the Jewish faith; it was through baptism that he entered into that faith.

By Christian baptism, individuals entered into Christ. The early Christians looked on baptism as something which produced a real union with Christ. Of course, in a missionary situation where people were coming direct from the old religion, baptism was for the most part adult baptism, and an adult would naturally have an experience that a child could not have. But, just as the Jewish convert was united with the Jewish faith, the Christian convert was united with Christ in a very real sense (cf. Romans 6:3ff.; Colossians 2:12). Baptism was not simply something that was done to the outside of the person; it was a real union with Christ.

Paul goes on to say that they had put on Christ. There may be a reference here to a custom which certainly existed later. The candidates for baptism were clothed in pure white robes, symbolic of the new life into which they entered. Just as the initiates put on their new white robes, their lives were clothed with Christ.

The result is that in the Church there was no difference between any of the members; they had all become children of God. In verse 28, Paul says that the distinction between Jew and Greek, slave and free, male and female is wiped out. There is something of very great interest here. In the Jewish morning prayer, which Paul must have used all his pre-Christian life, a Jewish man thanks God that 'You have not made me a Gentile, a slave or a woman.' Paul takes that prayer and reverses it. The old distinctions have gone; all are now one in Christ.

We have already seen (verse 16) that Paul interprets the promises made to Abraham as especially finding their fulfilment in Christ; and, if we are one with Christ, we, too, inherit the promises – and this great privilege comes not by a legalistic keeping of the law, but by an act of faith in the free grace of God.

Only one thing can wipe out the increasingly sharp distinctions and separations between individuals and between peoples: when all are debtors to God's grace and all are in Christ, only then will all be one. It is not human effort but the love of God which alone can unite a disunited world.

THE DAYS OF CHILDHOOD

Galatians 4:1–7

> This is what I mean: so long as the heir is an infant there is no difference between him and a slave, although he is owner of everything, but he is under the control of stewards and overseers until the day which his father has fixed arrives. It is just the same with us. When we were infants, we were in subjection to the elementary knowledge which this world can supply. But, when the fullness of time came, God sent forth his Son, born of a woman, born under the law, in order that he might redeem those who were subject to the law, so that we might be adopted as sons. Because you are sons, God sent forth the Spirit of his Son into our hearts, crying: 'Abba! Father!' The consequence is that you are no longer a slave but a son; and, if a son, an heir because God made you so.

In the ancient world, the process of growing up was much more clearly defined than it is today.

(1) In the Jewish world, on the first Sabbath after a boy had passed his 12th birthday, his father took him to the synagogue, where he became *a son of the law*. At that point, the father said a blessing: 'Blessed are you, O God, who has

taken from me the responsibility for this boy.' The boy prayed a prayer in which he said: 'O my God and God of my fathers! On this solemn and sacred day, which marks my passage from boyhood to manhood, I humbly raise my eyes to you, and declare, with sincerity and truth, that henceforth I will keep your commandments, and undertake and bear the responsibility of my actions towards you.' There was a clear dividing line in the boy's life; almost overnight he became a man.

(2) In Greece, a boy was under his father's care from the age of 7 until he was 18. He then became what was called an *ephebos*, which may be translated as *cadet*, and for two years he was under the direction of the state. The Athenians were divided into ten *phratriai*, or *clans*. Before a boy became an *ephebos*, at a festival called the *Apatouria*, he was received into the clan; and in a ceremonial act his long hair was cut off and offered to the gods. Once again, growing up was quite a distinct process.

(3) Under Roman law, the year at which a boy grew up was not definitely fixed, but it was always between the ages of 14 and 17. At a sacred festival in the family called the *Liberalia*, he took off the *toga praetexta*, which was a toga with a narrow purple band at the foot of it, and put on the *toga virilis*, which was a plain toga worn by adults. He was then escorted by his friends and relatives down to the forum and formally introduced to public life. It was essentially a religious ceremony. Once again, there was a quite definite day on which the boy attained manhood. There was a Roman custom that, on the day a boy or girl grew up, they offered their toys to Apollo to show that they had put away childish things.

When a boy was an *infant* in the eyes of the law, he might be the owner of a vast property, but he could take no legal decision; he was not in control of his own life; everything was done and directed for him; and, therefore, for all practical purposes he had no more freedom than if he were a slave; but, when he became a man, he entered into his full inheritance.

So – Paul argues – in the childhood of the world, the law was in control. But the law was only elementary knowledge. To describe it, Paul uses the word *stoicheia*. A *stoicheion* was originally a line of things; for instance, it can mean a line of soldiers. But it came to mean any elementary knowledge, like the teaching of the alphabet to children.

It has another meaning which some would see here – the elements of which the world is composed, and, in particular, the stars. The ancient world was haunted by a belief in astrology. If an individual was born under a certain star, that person's fate, they believed, was settled. People lived under the tyranny of the stars and longed for release. Some scholars think that Paul is saying that at one time the Galatians had been tyrannized by their belief in the evil and threatening influence of the stars. But the whole passage seems to make it necessary to take *stoicheia* in the sense of basic knowledge.

Paul says that when the Galatians – and indeed all men and women – were mere children, they were under the tyranny of the law; then, when everything was ready, Christ came and released them from that tyranny. So, now they are no longer slaves of the law; they have become heirs and have entered into their inheritance. The childhood which belonged to the law should be past; the freedom of adulthood has come.

The proof that we are God's children comes from the instinctive cry of the heart. In our deepest need, we cry: 'Father!' to God. Paul uses the double phrase, 'Abba! Father!'

Abba is the Aramaic word for *father*. It must have often been on Jesus' lips, and its sound was so sacred that the original language was retained. This instinctive cry of the heart Paul believes to be the work of the Holy Spirit. If our hearts cry out in this way, we know that we are God's children, and all the inheritance of grace is ours.

For Paul, those who governed their lives by slavery to the law were still children; those who had learned the way of grace had become mature in the Christian faith.

PROGRESS IN REVERSE

Galatians 4:8-11

> There was a time when you did not know God, and when you were slaves to gods who are no gods at all; but now that you know God – or rather now that God knows you – how can you turn back again to the weak and poverty-stricken elementary things, for it is to them that you wish to be enslaved all over again? You meticulously observe days and months and seasons and years. I am afraid for you, lest all the labour I spent on you is to go for nothing.

PAUL is still basing his thinking on the conception that the law is an elementary stage in religion, and that the mature adult is the person who takes a stand on grace. The law was all right in the old days when people did not know any better. But now they have come to know God and his grace. Then Paul corrects himself: we cannot by our own efforts know God; God reveals himself to us through his grace. We can never seek God unless he has already found us. So, Paul demands: 'Are you now going back to a stage that you should have left behind long ago?'

He calls the elementary things, the religion based on law, *weak and poverty-stricken*. (1) It is *weak* because it is helpless. It can define sin; it can convict a person of sin; but it can find neither forgiveness for past sin nor strength to conquer future sin. (2) It is *poverty-stricken* in comparison with the splendour of grace. By its very nature, the law can deal with only one situation. For every fresh situation, a fresh law is needed; but the wonder of grace is that it is *poikilos*, which means *variegated, many-coloured*. That is to say, there is no possible situation in life which grace cannot match; it is sufficient for all things.

One of the features of Jewish law was its observance of special times. In this passage, the *days* are the Sabbaths of each week; the *months* are the new moons; the *seasons* are the great annual feasts like the Passover, Pentecost and the Feast of Tabernacles; the *years* are the Sabbatic years, that is, every seventh year, which was a special year. The failure of a religion which is dependent on special occasions is that almost inevitably it divides days into sacred and secular; and the further almost inevitable step is that, when people have meticulously observed the sacred days, they are liable to think that they have discharged their duty to God.

Although that was the religion of legalism, it was very far from being the prophetic religion. It has been said that 'The ancient Hebrew people had no word in their language to correspond to the word "religion" as it is commonly used today. The whole of life as they saw it came from God, and was subject to his law and governance. There could be no separate part of it in their thought labelled "religion". Jesus Christ did not say: "I am come that they may have religion," but: "I am come that they may have life, and have it abundantly."' To make religion a thing of special times is to treat it as something that is external to life. For real Christians, every day is God's day.

It was Paul's fear that those who had once known the splendour of grace would slip back to legalism, and that men and women who had once lived in the presence of God would only think of God on special days.

LOVE'S APPEAL

Galatians 4:12–20

> Brothers, I entreat you: become as I am, because I became as you are. I have no complaints against the way that once you treated me. You know that it was because I was ill that I first preached the gospel to you. It must have been a temptation to you to do so, but you did not look on me with contempt or turn with loathing from me, but you received me as if I were an angel of God, as you would have received Christ Jesus. I once had cause to congratulate you. Where has that cause gone to? I am prepared to give evidence in your favour that you would have dug out your eyes and given them to me. So then – have I become your enemy because I tell you the truth? It is not for any honourable reason that these other people pay court to you, but because they wish to put the barriers up so that you will have to pay court to them. It is always a fine thing to be zealous in a fine affair, and that not only when I am actually present with you. My little children, for whom I suffer the birth-pangs all over again, until you have taken the form of Christ, I wish I could be with you now! I wish that I had not to talk like this to you, because I am worried about you.

PAUL makes not a theological but a personal appeal. He reminds them that for their sake he had become a Gentile; he had cut himself off from the traditions in which he had been brought up and become what they are; and his appeal is that they should not seek to become Jews but might become like himself.

Here we have a reference to Paul's 'thorn in the flesh'. It was through illness that he first came to them. We discuss this thorn more fully when dealing with 2 Corinthians 12:7. It has been held to be the persecution which he suffered, or the temptations of the flesh, which he is said never to have succeeded in suppressing, or his physical appearance, which the Corinthians regarded as contemptible (2 Corinthians 10:10). The oldest tradition is that it was violent headaches. From this passage itself, there emerge two indications.

The Galatians would have given him their eyes if they could have done so. It has been suggested that Paul's eyes always troubled him because he had been dazzled so much on the Damascus road that afterwards he could see only dimly and painfully.

The word translated as *you did not turn from me with loathing* literally means *you did not spit at me*. In the ancient world, it was the custom to spit when encountering an epileptic in order to avert the influence of the evil spirit which was believed to be resident in the sufferer; so, it has been suggested that Paul was an epileptic.

If we can find out just when Paul came to Galatia, it may be possible to deduce why he came. It is possible that Acts 13:13–14 describes that coming. That passage presents a problem. Paul, Barnabas and Mark had come from Cyprus to the mainland. They came to Perga in Pamphylia; there Mark left them; and then they proceeded straight to Antioch in Pisidia, which is in the province of Galatia. Why did Paul not preach in Pamphylia? It was a heavily populated district. Why did he choose to go to Antioch in Pisidia? The road that led there, up into the central plateau, was one of the most difficult and dangerous in the world. That is perhaps why Mark went home. Why, then, this sudden flight from Pamphylia? The reason may well be that, since Pamphylia and the coastal plain were districts where malarial fever raged, Paul contracted this sickness and his only remedy would be to seek the highlands of Galatia, so that he arrived among the Galatians a sick man. Now, this malaria recurs and is accompanied by a severe headache which has been likened to 'a red-hot bar thrust through the forehead'. It may well have been that it was this acute pain which was Paul's thorn in the flesh and which was torturing him when he first came to Galatia.

He talks about those who were deliberately being attentive to and making much of the Galatians; he means those who were seeking to persuade them to adopt Jewish ways. If they were successful, the Galatians would in turn have to seek approval from them in order to be allowed to be circumcised and enter the Jewish nation. The sole purpose behind this flattery was to get control of the Galatians and reduce them to subjection to themselves and to the law.

In the end, Paul uses a vivid metaphor. Bringing the Galatians to Christ cost him pain like the pain of childbirth; and now he has to go through it all again. Christ is in them, as it were in embryo; he has to bring them to birth.

No one can fail to see the deep affection of the last words. *My little children* – diminutives in Latin and Greek always express deep affection. John often uses this expression, but Paul uses it nowhere else; his heart is running over with emotion. We do well to note that Paul did not scold with bitter words; he had nothing but affectionate concern for his straying children. It was said of Florence Allshorn, the famous missionary and teacher, that if she had cause to rebuke any of her students she did so, as it were, with her arm around them. The accent of love will penetrate where the tones of anger will never find a way.

AN OLD STORY AND A NEW MEANING

Galatians 4:21–5:1

Tell me this – you who want to be subject to the law, you listen to it being read to you, don't you? Well, then, it stands written in it that Abraham had two sons; one was the son of the slave girl and one was the son of the free woman. But the son of the slave girl was born in the ordinary human way, whereas the son of the free woman was born through a promise. Now, these things are an allegory. For these two women stand for two covenants. One of these covenants – the one which originated on Mount Sinai – bears children who are destined for slavery – and that one is represented by Hagar. Now, Hagar stands for Mount Sinai, which is in Arabia, and corresponds to the present Jerusalem; for she is a slave and so are her children. But the Jerusalem which is above is free and she is our mother. For it stands written: 'Rejoice, O barren one, who never bore a child; break forth into a shout of joy, O you who know not the pangs of bearing a child; for the children of her who was left alone are more than those of her who had a husband.' But we, brothers, are in the same position as Isaac; we are children of promise. But in the old days the child who was born in the ordinary human way persecuted the child who was born in the spiritual way; and exactly the same thing happens now. But what does the Scripture say? 'Cast out the slave girl and her son, for the son of the slave girl must not inherit with the son of the free woman.' So we, brothers, are children not of the slave girl but of the free woman. It is for this freedom that Christ has set us free. Stand, therefore, in it and do not get yourselves involved all over again in a slavish yoke.

WHEN we attempt to interpret a passage like this, we must remember that, for devout and scholarly Jews, and especially for the Rabbis, Scripture had more than one meaning; and the literal meaning was often regarded as the least important. For the Jewish Rabbis, a passage of Scripture had four meanings. (1) *Peshat*, its simple or literal meaning. (2) *Remaz*, its suggested meaning. (3) *Derush*, the meaning deduced by investigation. (4) *Sod*, the allegorical meaning. The first letters of these four words – P R D S – are the consonants of the word *Paradise*; and, when a Rabbi had succeeded in penetrating into these four different meanings, he reached the joy of paradise.

It is to be noted that the summit of all meanings was the *allegorical* meaning. It therefore often happened that the Rabbis would take a simple bit of historical narrative from the Old Testament and read into it inner meanings which often appear to us fantastic but which were very convincing to the people of their day. Paul was a trained Rabbi; and that is what he is doing here. He takes the story involving Abraham, Sarah, Hagar, Ishmael and Isaac (Genesis 16, 17, 21), which in the Old Testament is a straightforward narrative, and he turns it into an allegory to illustrate his point.

The outline of the story is as follows: Abraham and Sarah had both reached an advanced age, and Sarah had no child. She did what any wife would have done in those patriarchal times and sent Abraham in to her slave girl, Hagar, to see if she could bear a child on her behalf. Hagar had a son called

Ishmael. In the meantime, God had come and promised that Sarah would have a child, which was so difficult to believe that it appeared impossible to Abraham and Sarah; but in due time Isaac was born. That is to say, Ishmael was born as a result of the ordinary human instincts and urges; Isaac was born because of God's promise; and Sarah was a free woman, while Hagar was a slave girl. From the beginning, Hagar had been inclined to gloat over Sarah, because barrenness was a matter of great shame to a woman; there was an atmosphere charged with trouble. Later, Sarah found Ishmael 'mocking' (Authorized Version) Isaac – this Paul equates with persecution – and insisted that Hagar should be cast out, so that the child of the slave girl should not share the inheritance with her freeborn son. Further, Arabia was regarded as the land of slaves where the descendants of Hagar lived.

Paul takes that old story and allegorizes it. Hagar stands for the old covenant of the law, made on Mount Sinai, which is in fact in Arabia, the land of Hagar's descendants. Hagar herself was a slave, and all her children were born into slavery; and that covenant whose basis is the law turns men and women into slaves of the law. Hagar's child was born from merely human instincts; and legalism is the best that human beings can do. On the other hand, Sarah stands for the new covenant in Jesus Christ, God's new way of dealing with us not by law but by grace. Her child was born free, and all his descendants must be free; he was the child not simply of human desire but of the promise of God. As the child of the slave girl persecuted the child of the free woman, the children of law now persecute the children of grace and promise. But, as in the end the child of the slave girl was cast out and had no share in the inheritance, so in the end those who are legalists will be cast out from God and have no share in the inheritance of grace.

Strange as all this may seem to us, it contains one great truth. Those who make law the principle of their lives are in the position of slaves; whereas those who make grace the principle of their lives are free, for, as St Augustine put it, the Christian's maxim is: 'Love God, and do what you like.' It is the power of that love, and not the constraint of law, that will keep us right; for love is always more powerful than law.

THE PERSONAL RELATIONSHIP

Galatians 5:2–12

> Look now – it is I, Paul, who am speaking to you – I tell you that if you get yourself circumcised Christ is no good to you. Again I give my word to every man who gets himself circumcised that he is under obligation to keep the whole law. You who seek to get yourselves right with God by means of legalism have got yourself into a position in which you have rendered ineffective all that Christ did for you. You have fallen from grace. For it is by the Spirit and by faith that we eagerly expect the hope of being right with God. For in Jesus Christ it is not of the slightest importance whether a man is circumcised or uncircumcised. What does matter is faith which works through love. You were running well. Who put up a road-block to stop you obeying the truth? The persuasion which is being exercised on you just now is not from him who calls you. A little leaven leavens the whole lump. I have confidence in you in the Lord; I am sure that you will take no other view. He who is upsetting you – whoever he is – will bear his own judgment. As for me, brothers, if I am still preaching that circumcision is necessary, why am I still being persecuted? So the stumbling-block of the cross is

removed, is it? I wish that those who are upsetting you would get themselves not only circumcised but castrated!

I⟨T⟩ was Paul's position that the way of grace and the way of law were mutually exclusive. The way of law makes salvation dependent on human achievement; those who take the way of grace simply cast themselves and their sin upon the mercy of God. Paul went on to argue that if you accepted circumcision, that is to say, if you accepted one part of the law, logically you had to accept the whole law.

Suppose there are people who want to become naturalized citizens of a country and who carefully carry out all the rules and regulations of that country as these affect naturalization. They cannot stop there but are bound to accept *all* the other rules and regulations as well. So, Paul argued that if a man were circumcised he had put himself under an obligation to the whole law to which circumcision was the introduction; and, if he took that way, he had automatically turned his back on the way of grace, and, as far as he was concerned, Christ might never have died.

To Paul, all that mattered was faith, which works through love. That is just another way of saying that the essence of Christianity is not law but a personal relationship to Jesus Christ. The Christian faith is founded not on a book but on a person; its dynamic is not obedience to any law but love of Jesus Christ.

Once, the Galatians had known that; but now they were turning back to the law. 'A little leaven', said Paul, 'leavens the whole lump.' For the Jews, leaven nearly always stood for evil influence. What Paul is saying is: 'This legalistic movement may not have gone very far yet, but you must root it out before it destroys your whole religion.'

Paul ends with a very blunt saying. Galatia was near Phrygia, and the great worship of that part of the world was of Cybele. It was the practice that priests and really devout worshippers of Cybele mutilated themselves by castration. Paul says: 'If you go on in this way, of which circumcision is the beginning, you might as well end up by castrating yourselves like the priests of this goddess.' It is a grim illustration, at which we might raise our eyebrows; but it would be intensely real to the Galatians, who knew all about the priests of Cybele.

CHRISTIAN FREEDOM

Galatians 5:13-15

> As for you, brothers, it was for freedom that you were called, only you must not use this freedom as a bridgehead through which the worst side of human nature can invade you, but in love you must serve one another; for the whole law stands complete in one word, in the sentence: 'You must love your neighbour as yourself.' But if you snap at one another, and devour one another, you must watch that you do not end up by wiping each other out.

WITH this paragraph, Paul's letter changes its emphasis. Up to this point it has been theological; now it becomes intensely ethical. Paul had a characteristically practical mind. Even when he has been scaling the highest heights of thought, he always ends a letter on a practical note. To him, a theology was not the slightest use unless it could be lived out. In Romans, he wrote one of the world's great theological treatises; and then, quite suddenly, in chapter 12 the theology came down to earth and developed into the most practical advice. The New Testament scholar Vincent Taylor once said: 'The test of a good theologian is, can he write a tract?' That is to say, after all the flights of thought, can a theologian reduce it all to something that the ordinary person can understand and do? Paul always triumphantly satisfies that test, just as here the whole matter is brought to the acid test of daily living.

Paul's theology always ran one danger. When he declared that the end of the reign of law had come and that the reign of grace had arrived, it was always possible for someone to say: 'That, then, means that I can do what I like; all the restraints are lifted and I can follow my inclinations wherever they lead me. Law is gone, and grace ensures forgiveness anyway.' But, for Paul, there were always two obligations. (1) One he does not mention here, but it is implicit in all his thinking. It is *the obligation to God*. If God loved us like that, then the love of Christ puts us under constraint. I cannot bring discredit to a life which God paid for with his own life. (2) There is the *obligation to our neighbours*. We are free, but our freedom loves its neighbour as itself.

The names of the different forms of government are significant. *Monarchy* is government by one, and began in the interests of efficiency, for government by committees has always had its drawbacks. *Oligarchy* means government by the few and can be justified by arguing that only the few are fit to govern. *Aristocracy* means government by the best, but *best* is left to be defined. *Plutocracy* means government by the wealthy and is justified by the claim that those who have the biggest stake in the country have a logical right to rule it. *Democracy* means government of the people, by the people, for the people. Christianity is the only true democracy, because in a Christian state all citizens would think as much of their neighbours as they do of themselves. Christian freedom is not licence, for the simple but tremendous reason that Christians are not men and women who have become free to sin, but people who, by the grace of God, have become free *not to sin*.

Paul adds a grim bit of advice. 'Unless', he says, 'you solve the problem of living together, you will make life impossible.' Selfishness in the end does not bring people respect; it destroys them.

THE EVIL THINGS

Galatians 5:16–21

> I tell you, let your walk and conversation be dominated by the Spirit, and don't let the desires of the lower side of your nature have their way. For the desires of the lower side of human nature are the very reverse of the desires of the Spirit, and the desires of the Spirit are the very reverse of those of the lower side of human nature, for these are fundamentally opposed to each other, so that you cannot do whatever you like. The deeds of the lower side of human nature are obvious – fornication, impurity, wantonness, idolatry, witchcraft, enmity, strife, jealousy, uncontrolled temper, self-seeking, dissension, heretical division, envy, drunkenness, carousing, and all that is like these things. I warn you, as I have warned you before, that those who do things like that will not inherit the kingdom of God.

No one was ever more conscious of the tension in human nature than Paul. As the soldier in Studdert Kennedy's poem said:

> I'm a man and a man's a mixture
> Right down from his very birth;

For part of him comes from heaven,
And part of him comes from earth.

For Paul, it was essential that Christian freedom should
mean not freedom to indulge the lower side of human nature,
but freedom to walk in the life of the Spirit. He gives us a
catalogue of evil things. Every word he uses has a picture
behind it.

Fornication: it has been said, and said truly, that the one
completely new virtue Christianity brought into the world
was chastity. Christianity came into a world where sexual
immorality was not only condoned, but was regarded as an
essential part of everyday life.

Impurity: the word that Paul uses (*akatharsia*) is interesting. It can be used for the pus of an unclean wound, for a
tree that has never been pruned, for material which has never
been sorted. In its positive form (*katharos*, an adjective
meaning *pure*), it is commonly used in housing contracts to
describe a house that is left clean and in good condition. But
its most significant use is that *katharos* is used of that
ceremonial cleanness which entitles people to approach their
gods. Impurity, then, is that which makes people unfit to come
before God, the contamination of life with the things which
separate us from him.

Wantonness: this word (*aselgeia*) is translated as *licen-
tiousness* in the Revised Standard Version (Mark 7:22; 2
Corinthians 12:21; Galatians 5:19; Ephesians 4:19; 1 Peter
4:3; Jude 4; Romans 13:13 and 2 Peter 2:18). It has been
defined as 'readiness for any pleasure'. Those who practise it
have been said to know no restraint, but to do whatever any
whim and wanton lack of respect may suggest. The Jewish
historian Josephus ascribed it to Queen Jezebel when she built
a temple to Baal in Jerusalem. The idea is of people who are

so bound up in their own desire that they have ceased to care what others say or think.

Idolatry: this means the worship of gods which human hands have made. It is the sin in which material things have taken the place of God.

Witchcraft: this literally means *the use of drugs*. It can mean the healing use of drugs by a doctor; but it can also mean *poisoning*, and it came to be especially connected with the use of drugs for sorcery, of which the ancient world was full.

Enmity: the idea is that of the individual who is characteristically hostile to other people; it is the precise opposite of the virtue of the love of Christians for one another and for all people.

Strife: originally, this word had mainly to do with *the rivalry for prizes*. It can even be used in a good sense in that connection, but much more commonly it means the rivalry which has resulted in quarrelling and wrangling.

Jealousy: this word (*zelos*, from which our word *zeal* comes) was originally a good word. It meant *emulation*, the desire to attain to nobility when we see it. But it degenerated; it came to mean the desire to have what someone else has, wrong desire for what is not ours.

Uncontrolled temper: the word Paul uses means bursts of temper. It describes not an anger which lasts but anger which flares up and then dies.

Self-seeking: this word has a very illuminating history. It is *eritheia* and originally meant *the work of a hired labourer* (*erithos*). So it came to mean *work done for pay*. It went on to mean *canvassing for political or public office*, and it describes the person who wants office, not from any motives of service, but for what can be got out of it.

Dissension: literally the word means *a standing apart*. After one of his great victories, the British Admiral Lord

Nelson attributed it to the fact that he had the happiness to command 'a band of brothers'. *Dissension* describes a society in which the very opposite is the case, where the members fly apart instead of coming together.

Heretical division: this might be described as clearly focused disagreement. The word is *hairesis*, from which comes our word *heresy*. *Hairesis* was originally not a bad word at all. It comes from a root which means *to choose*, and it was used for a philosopher's school of followers or for any group of people who shared a common belief. The tragedy of life is that people who hold different views very often end up by disliking not each other's views but each other. It should be possible to hold different views and yet remain friends.

Envy: this word (*phthonos*) is a mean word. The Greek dramatist Euripides called it 'the greatest of all diseases'. The essence of it is that it does not describe the spirit which desires, nobly or ignobly, to have what someone else has; it describes the spirit which grudges the fact that the other person has these things at all. It does not so much want the things for itself; it merely wants to take them from the other. The Stoics defined it as 'grief at someone else's good'. The fourth-century Church father Basil the Great called it 'grief at your neighbour's good fortune'. It is the quality not so much of the jealous but rather of the embittered mind.

Drunkenness: in the ancient world, this was not a common vice. The Greeks drank more wine than they did milk; even children drank wine. But they drank it in the proportion of three parts of water to two of wine. Both Greeks and Christians would have condemned drunkenness as a thing which turned people into animals.

Carousing: this word (*komos*) has an interesting history. A *komos* was a group of friends who accompanied a victor of the games after his victory. They danced and laughed and sang his praises. It also described the devotees of Bacchus, god of wine. It describes what in England in the early decades of the nineteenth century would have been called a *rout*. It means unrestrained revelry, enjoyment that has degenerated and is out of control.

When we get to the root meaning of these words, we see that life has not changed so very much.

THE LOVELY THINGS

Galatians 5:22–6

> But the fruit of the Spirit is love, joy, peace, patience, kindness, goodness, fidelity, gentleness, self-control. There is no law which condemns things like that. Those who belong to Jesus Christ have crucified their own unregenerate selves along with all their passions and their desires.
>
> If we are living in the Spirit, let us also keep step with the Spirit. Don't become seekers after empty reputation; don't provoke each other; don't envy each other.

As in the previous verses Paul set out the evil things characteristic of the flesh, the lower side of human nature, so now he sets out the lovely things which are the fruit of the Spirit. Again it is worth while to look at each word separately.

Love: the New Testament word for *love* is *agape*. This is not a word which is commonly used in classical Greek. In Greek, there are four words for love. (1) *Eros* means the love between the sexes; it is the love which has passion in it. It is never used in the New Testament at all. (2) *Philia* is the warm love which we feel for our nearest and dearest; it is love from the heart. (3) *Storgē* rather means affection and is especially used of the love of parents and children. (4) *Agape*, the Christian word, means unconquerable benevolence. It means that, no matter what people may do to us by way of insult or injury or humiliation, we will never seek anything else but their highest good. It is therefore a feeling of the mind as much as of the heart; it concerns the will as much as the emotions. It describes the deliberate effort – which we can make only with the help of God – never to seek anything but the best even for those who seek the worst for us.

Joy: the Greek is *chara*, and the characteristic of this word is that it most often describes that joy which has a basis in religion (cf. Psalm 30:11; Romans 14:17, 15:13; Philippians 1:4, 1:25). It is not the joy that comes from earthly things, still less from triumphing over someone else in competition. It is a joy whose foundation is God.

Peace: in contemporary colloquial Greek, this word (*eirene*) had two interesting usages. It was used of the serenity which a country enjoyed under the just and generous government of a good emperor; and it was used of the good order of a town or village. Villages had an official who was called the superintendent of the village's *eirene*, the keeper of the public peace. Usually in the New Testament, *eirene* stands for the Hebrew *shalom* and means not just freedom from trouble but everything that makes for a person's highest good. Here, it means that tranquillity of heart which derives from the all-pervading consciousness that our times are in the hands of God. It is interesting to note that *Chara* and *Eirene* both became very common Christian names in the Church.

Patience: the Greek word used is *makrothumia*. This is a great word. The writer of 1 Maccabees (8:4) says that it was by *makrothumia* that the Romans gained control of the world, and by that he means the Roman persistence which would never make peace with an enemy even in defeat, a kind of conquering patience. Generally speaking, the word is used of patience not in relation to things or events but in relation to people. The fourth-century bishop and preacher John Chrysostom said that it is the grace of those who could revenge themselves and do not, people who are slow to anger. The most illuminating thing about it is that it is commonly used in the New Testament of the attitude of God towards men and women (Romans 2:4, 9:22; 1 Timothy 1:16; 1 Peter 3:20). If God had been like us, he would have wiped out this world long ago; but he has that patience which puts up with all our sinning and will not reject us. In our dealings with one another, we must reproduce this loving, forbearing, forgiving, patient attitude of God towards ourselves.

Kindness and *goodness* are closely connected words. For *kindness*, the word is *chrestotes*. It, too, is commonly translated as *goodness*. The Rheims version of 2 Corinthians 6:6 translates it as *sweetness*. It is a lovely word. The Greek historian and philosopher Plutarch says that it has a far wider place than justice. Old wine is called *chrestos*, *mellow*. Christ's yoke is called *chrestos* (Matthew 11:30), that is, it does not cause discomfort or irritation. The whole idea of the word is a goodness which is kind. The word Paul uses for *goodness* (*agathosune*) is a word peculiar to the Bible and does not occur in secular Greek (Romans 15:14; Ephesians 5:9; 2 Thessalonians 1:11). It is the widest word for goodness; it is defined as 'virtue equipped at every point'. What is the difference? *Agathosune* might, and could, rebuke and discipline; *chrestotes* can only help. The nineteenth-century Bishop of Dublin, R. C. Trench, says that Jesus showed *agathosune* when he cleansed the Temple and drove out those who were making it a bazaar; but he showed *chrestotes* when he was kind to the sinning woman who anointed his feet. Christians need that goodness which at one and the same time can be kind and strong.

Fidelity: this word (*pistis*) is common in secular Greek for *trustworthiness*. It is the characteristic of people who are reliable.

Gentleness: *praotes* is the most untranslatable of words. In the New Testament, it has three main meanings. (1) It means *being submissive to the will of God* (Matthew 5:5, 11:29, 21:5). (2) It means *being teachable*, being not too proud to learn (James 1:21). (3) Most often of all, it means *being considerate* (1 Corinthians 4:21; 2 Corinthians 10:1; Ephesians 4:2). Aristotle defined *praotes* as the mid-point between excessive anger and excessive angerlessness, the quality of the person who is always angry at the right time and never at the wrong time. What throws most light on its meaning is that the adjective *praus* is used of an animal that has been tamed and brought under control; and so the word speaks of that self-control which Christ alone can give.

Self-control: the word is *egkrateia*, which Plato uses of *self-mastery*. It is the spirit which has overcome and controlled its desires and its love of pleasure. It is used of the athlete's discipline of the body (1 Corinthians 9:25) and of the Christian's control of sex (1 Corinthians 7:9). Secular Greek uses it of the virtue of an emperor who never lets his private interests influence the government of his people. It is the virtue which enables people to have such control of themselves that they are fit to be the servants of others.

It was Paul's belief and experience that Christians died with Christ and rose again to a life, new and clean, in which the evil things of the old self were gone and the lovely things of the Spirit had come to fruition.

BURDEN-BEARING

Galatians 6:1-5

> Brothers, if a man is caught out in some moral slip-up,
> you whose lives are dominated by the Spirit must correct
> such a man with the spirit of gentleness, and, as you do
> it, you must think about yourselves, in case you too
> should be tempted. Carry one another's burdens, and
> so fulfil the law of Christ. For, if anyone thinks of
> himself as important while he is of no importance, he is
> deceiving himself with the fancies of his mind. Let every
> man test his own work, and then any ground of boasting
> that he has will be in regard to himself and not in
> comparison with others. For each man must carry his
> own pack.

PAUL knew the problems that arise in any Christian society.
The best people can slip up. The word Paul uses (*paraptōma*)
does not mean a deliberate sin; but a slip that might come to
someone on an icy road or a dangerous path. Now, the danger
of those who are really trying to live the Christian life is that
they are apt to judge the sins of others harshly. There is an
element of hardness in many good people. There are many
good people to whom you could not go and sob out a story of
failure and defeat; they would be bleakly unsympathetic. But
Paul says that, if people do slip, the real Christian duty is to
get them on their feet again. The word he uses for *to correct*
is used for making a repair and also for the work of a surgeon
in removing some growth or in setting a broken limb. The
whole atmosphere of the word lays the stress not on
punishment but on cure; the correction is thought of not as a
penalty but as putting something right. And Paul goes on to
say that when we see someone make a mistake we do well to
say: 'There but for the grace of God go I.'

He goes on to rebuke conceit and gives a recipe whereby it may well be avoided. We are to compare our achievement not with the work of our neighbours but with what our best would have been. When we do that, there can never be any cause for conceit.

Twice in this passage, Paul speaks about bearing burdens. There is a kind of burden which comes to people from the chances and the changes of life; it is fulfilling the law of Christ to help everyone who has such a burden to carry. But there are also burdens which people must bear for themselves. The word Paul uses for this kind of burden is the word for a soldier's pack. There is a duty which no one else can do for us and a task for which we must be personally responsible.

KEEPING IT UP

Galatians 6:6–10

> He who is being instructed in the word must share in all good things with him who is giving instruction. Don't deceive yourselves; no one can make a fool of God; whatever a man sows, this he will also reap. He who sows to his own lower nature will from that nature reap a blighted harvest. He who sows to the Spirit will from the Spirit reap life eternal. Don't get tired of doing the fine thing; for, when the proper time comes, we will reap so long as we don't relax our efforts. So then, as we have opportunity, let us do good to all, especially to those who are members of the household of the faith.

HERE, Paul becomes intensely practical.

The Christian Church had its teachers. In those days, the Church was in a very real way a sharing institution. No

Christian could bear to have too much while others had too little. So Paul says: 'If someone is teaching you the eternal truths, the least you can do is share with that person such material things as you possess.'

He goes on to state a grim truth. He insists that life holds the scales with an even balance. If we allow the lower side of our nature to dominate us, in the end we can expect nothing but a harvest of trouble. But, if we keep on walking the high way and doing the fine thing, in the end God will repay.

Christianity never took the threat out of life. The Greeks believed in the goddess of retribution, Nemesis; they believed that, when people did wrong, immediately Nemesis was on their trail and sooner or later caught up. All Greek tragedy is a sermon on the text: 'The doer shall suffer.' What we do not always remember is this: it is blessedly true that God can and does forgive us for our sins, but not even he can wipe out the consequence of sin. If people sin against their bodies, sooner or later they will pay in ruined health – even if they are forgiven. If people sin against their loved ones, sooner or later hearts will be broken – even if they are forgiven. John B. Gough, the great temperance orator, who had lived a reckless early life, used to declare in warning: 'The scars remain.' And Origen, the great third-century Christian scholar and a universalist, believed that, although all would be saved, even then the marks of sin would remain. We cannot trade on the forgiveness of God. There is a moral law in the universe. If we break it, we may be forgiven; but, nonetheless, we break it at our peril.

Paul finishes by reminding his friends that sometimes the duty of generosity may be very trying, but – as Ecclesiastes tells us (11:1) – no one who ever cast bread upon the waters found that it did not some day return.

THE CLOSING WORDS

Galatians 6:11–18

> See in what large letters I am writing in my own hand-writing. Those who wish to make a pretentious display from the merely human point of view are trying to compel you to get yourselves circumcised, but their real object is to avoid persecution because of the cross of Christ. For those who advocate circumcision do not themselves keep the law, but they wish you to get yourselves circumcised that they may boast about the way in which you are observing the outward and the human rituals. God forbid that I should boast except in the cross of our Lord Jesus Christ through whom the world has been crucified to me and I to the world. To be circumcised is of no importance, and to be un-circumcised makes no difference. What does matter is to be re-created. May peace and mercy be upon all who shall walk by this standard and on the Israel of God. For the future, let no one trouble me, for I bear the brands of Jesus in my body.
>
> Brothers, the grace of the Lord Jesus Christ be with your spirit. So let it be.

USUALLY, Paul added only his signature to the letter which the scribe wrote to his dictation; but in this case his heart is running over with such love and anxiety for the Galatians that he writes this whole last paragraph. 'See', he says, 'in what large letters I am writing in my own handwriting.' The large letters may be due to three things. (1) This paragraph may be written large because of its importance, as if it were printed in bold type. (2) It may be written large because Paul was not used to writing with a pen, and it was the best that he could do. (3) It may be that Paul's eyes were weak, or that he was suffering from a blinding headache, and all he could produce was the large, sprawling handwriting of someone who could hardly see.

He comes back to the central point. Those who wanted the Galatians to get themselves circumcised did so for three reasons. (1) It would save them from persecution. The Romans recognized the Jewish religion and officially allowed Jews to practise it. Circumcision was the indisputable mark of a Jew; and so these people saw in it a passport to safety should persecution arise. Circumcision would keep them safe from both the hatred of the Jews and the law of Rome. (2) In the last analysis, by circumcision and by keeping the rules and regulations of the law, they were trying to put on a show that would win the approval of God. Paul, however, was quite certain that nothing that individuals could achieve for themselves could win salvation; so, once again, pointing them to the cross, he summons them to stop trying to earn salvation and to trust to the grace which loved them like that. (3) Those who wanted the Galatians to be circumcised did not themselves keep all the law. No one could. But they wanted to boast about the Galatians as their latest conquests. They wanted to glory in their power over people whom they had reduced to their own legalistic slavery. So, Paul once again lays it down with all the intensity of which he is capable that circumcision and uncircumcision do not matter; what does matter is that act of faith in Christ which opens up a new life.

'I bear', said Paul, 'the brands of Jesus in my body.' There are two possible meanings of this.

(1) The *stigmata* have always fascinated people. It is told of Francis of Assisi that once, as he fasted on a lonely mountain top, he seemed to see the love of God crucified on a cross that stretched across the whole horizon, and as he saw it a sword of grief and pity pierced his heart. Slowly the vision faded, and Francis relaxed; and then, they say, he

looked down and there were the marks of the nails in his hands, marks that he bore for the rest of his life. Whether it is truth or legend we cannot tell, for there are more things in this world than our matter-of-fact philosophy dreams of; and some think that Paul had passed through an experience of crucifixion with his Lord so real that he, too, bore the prints of the nails in his hands.

(2) Often a master branded his slaves with a mark that showed them to be his. Most probably, what Paul means is that the scars of the things he had suffered for Christ are the brands which show him to be Christ's slave. In the end, it is not his apostolic authority that he uses as a basis of appeal; it is the wounds he sustained for Christ's sake. Like Mr Valiant-for-Truth, in John Bunyan's *The Pilgrim's Progress*, Paul said: 'My marks and scars I carry with me to be my witness to him who will now be my rewarder.'

After the storm and stress and intensity of the letter comes the peace of the benediction. Paul has argued and rebuked and cajoled; but his last word is *grace*, for him the only word that really mattered.

The Letter to the Ephesians

INTRODUCTION TO THE
LETTER TO THE EPHESIANS

The Supreme Letter

By common consent, the Letter to the Ephesians ranks very high in the devotional and theological literature of the Christian Church. It has been called 'the Queen of the Epistles' – and rightly so. Many would hold that it is indeed the highest reach of New Testament thought. When the great Scottish Protestant reformer John Knox was very near to death, the book that was most often read to him was John Calvin's *Sermons on the Letter to the Ephesians*. The poet Samuel Taylor Coleridge said of Ephesians that it was 'the divinest composition'. He went on: 'It embraces first, those doctrines peculiar to Christianity, and, then, those precepts common with it in natural religion.' Ephesians clearly has a unique place in the Pauline correspondence.

And yet there are certain very real problems connected with it. These problems are not the product of the minds of over-critical scholars, but are plain for all to see. When, however, these problems are solved, Ephesians becomes a greater letter than ever and shines with an even more radiant light.

The Circumstances behind the Writing of Ephesians

Before we turn to the doubtful things, let us set down the certainties. First, it is clear that Ephesians was written when

Paul was in prison. He calls himself 'a prisoner for Christ' (3:1); it is as 'a prisoner for the Lord' that he begs them (4:1); he is 'an ambassador in chains' (6:20). It was in prison, and very near to the end of his life, that Paul wrote Ephesians.

Second, Ephesians clearly has a close connection with Colossians. It would seem that Tychicus was the bearer of both these letters. In Colossians, Paul says that Tychicus will tell them all his news (Colossians 4:7); and in Ephesians he says that Tychicus will tell them everything about what he is doing (Ephesians 6:21). Further, there is a close resemblance between the substance of the two letters, so close that more than fifty-five verses in the two letters are word for word the same. Either, as Coleridge held, Colossians is what might be called 'the overflow' of Ephesians, or Ephesians is a greater version of Colossians. We shall in the end come to see that it is this resemblance which gives us the clue to the unique place of Ephesians among the letters of Paul.

The Problem

So, it is certain that Ephesians was written when Paul was in prison for the faith and that it has in some way the closest possible connection with Colossians. The problem emerges when we begin to examine the question of *to whom Ephesians was written*.

In the ancient world, letters were written on rolls of papyrus. When finished, they were tied with thread, and, if they were especially private or important, the knots in the thread were then sealed. But it was rare for any address to be written on them, for the very simple reason that, for the ordinary individual, there was no postal system. There was a government post, but it was available only for official and imperial correspondence and not for the ordinary person. Letters in those days were delivered by hand, and therefore no address was necessary. So, the titles of the New Testament letters are not part of the original letters at all. They were inserted afterwards when the letters were collected and published for all the Church to read.

When we study Ephesians closely, we find that it is extremely unlikely that it was written to the church at Ephesus. There are *internal* reasons for arriving at that conclusion.

(1) The letter was written to Gentiles. The recipients were 'Gentiles by birth, called "the uncircumcision" by those who are called "the circumcision" . . . at that time without Christ, being aliens from the commonwealth of Israel, and strangers to the covenants of promise' (2:11–12). Paul urges that they 'no longer live as the Gentiles live' (4:17). The fact that they were Gentiles did not of itself mean that the letter could not have been written to Ephesus; but it is something to note.

(2) Ephesians is the most impersonal letter Paul ever wrote. It is entirely without personal greetings and without the intimate personal messages of which the other letters are so full. That is doubly surprising when we remember that Paul spent longer in Ephesus than in any other city – no less than three years (Acts 20:31). Further, there is no more intimate and affectionate passage in the whole New Testament than Acts 20:17–35, where we have Paul's farewell talk to the elders of Ephesus, before he left Miletus on his last journey. It is very difficult to believe in the light of all this that Paul would have sent a letter to Ephesus which was so impersonal.

(3) The indication of the letter is that Paul and the recipients did not know each other personally and that their knowledge of each other came by hearsay. In 1:15, Paul writes: 'I have *heard* of your faith in the Lord Jesus.' The loyalty of the people to whom he was writing was not

something he had experienced but something about which he had been told. In 3:2, he writes to them: 'For surely you have already heard of the commission of God's grace that was given to me for you.' That is to say: 'Surely you have heard that God gave me the special task and office of being the apostle to Gentiles such as you.' The Church's knowledge of Paul as the apostle to the Gentiles was something of which they had heard, but not something which they knew by personal contact with him. So, within itself, the letter bears signs that it does not fit the close and personal relationship which Paul had with the church at Ephesus.

These facts might be explained; but there is one *external* fact which settles the matter. In 1:1, none of the great early manuscripts of the Greek New Testament contains the words *in Ephesus*. They all read: 'Paul . . . to the saints who are also faithful in Christ Jesus.' And we know, from the way in which they comment on it, that that was the form in which the early Greek fathers knew the text.

Was Paul the Author?

Some scholars have gone on to find still another difficulty in Ephesians. They have doubted whether Paul was the author of the letter at all. On what grounds do they base their doubts?

They say that the *vocabulary* is different from the vocabulary of Paul; and it is true that there are some seventy words in Ephesians which are not found in any other letter written by Paul. That need not trouble us, for the fact is that in Ephesians Paul was saying things which he had never said before. He was travelling a road of thought along which he had not travelled before; and naturally he needed new words to express new thoughts. It would be ridiculous to demand that someone with a mind like Paul's should never add to his vocabulary and should always express himself in the same way.

They say that the *style* is not the style of Paul. It is true – we can see it even in the English, let alone in the Greek – that the style of Ephesians is different from that of the other letters. The other letters are all written to meet a definite situation. But, as the New Testament scholar A. H. McNeile has said, Ephesians is 'a theological tract, or rather a religious meditation'. Even the use of language is different. Another scholar, James Moffatt, puts it this way: generally speaking, Paul's language pours out like a torrent; but in Ephesians we have 'a slow, bright stream, flowing steadily along, which brims its high banks'. The length of the sentences in Ephesians is astonishing. In the Greek, Ephesians 1:3–14, 1:15–23, 2:1–9 and 3:1–7 are each one long, meandering sentence. McNeile very beautifully and rightly calls Ephesians 'a poem in prose'. All this is very unlike Paul's normal style.

What is to be said in response to this? There is first the general fact that no great writer always writes in the same style. Shakespeare can produce the very different styles of *Hamlet*, *A Midsummer Night's Dream*, *The Taming of the Shrew* and the sonnets. Any great stylist – and Paul was a great stylist – writes in a style to fit the aim and the circumstances at the time of writing. It is bad criticism to say that Paul did not write Ephesians simply because he has developed a new vocabulary and a new style.

But there is more. Let us remember how Paul wrote most of his letters. He wrote them in the middle of a busy ministry, when, for the most part, he was on the road. He wrote them to meet a pressing problem which had to be dealt with at that precise moment. That is to say, in most of his letters Paul was writing against time. Now, let us remember that, if Paul wrote

Ephesians, he wrote it *when he was in prison* and therefore had all the time in the world to consider what he wrote. Is it any wonder that the style of Ephesians is not the style of the earlier letters?

Moreover, this difference in style, this meditative, poetical quality, is most apparent in the first three chapters, and they are *one long prayer*, culminating in a great hymn of praise to God. There is, in fact, nothing like this in all Paul's letters. This is the language of lyrical prayer, not the language of argument or controversy or rebuke.

The differences are a long way from proving that Ephesians is not by Paul.

The Thought of the Epistle

Certain scholars want to go on to say that the thought of Ephesians is beyond the thought of any of the other letters of Paul. Let us see what that thought is. We have seen that Ephesians is intimately connected with Colossians, whose central thought is *the all-sufficiency of Jesus Christ*. In Jesus Christ were hidden all the treasures of wisdom and knowledge (Colossians 2:3); all the fullness of God dwelt in him (Colossians 1:19); in him the whole fullness of deity dwells bodily (Colossians 2:9); he alone is necessary and sufficient for our salvation (Colossians 1:14). The whole thought of Colossians is based on the complete sufficiency of Jesus Christ.

The thought of Ephesians is a development of that idea. It is summarized in two verses of the first chapter, in which Paul speaks of God as having 'with all wisdom and insight . . . made known to us the mystery of his will, according to his good pleasure that he set forth in Christ, as a plan for the fullness of time, to gather up all things in him, things in heaven and things on earth' (Ephesians 1:9–10).

The key thought of Ephesians is the gathering together of all things in Jesus Christ. In nature as it is, without Christ there is nothing but disunity and disharmony; it is, as Tennyson described it, 'red in tooth and claw'. The dominion that human beings hold has broken the social union which should exist between them and the natural world; we are divided from one another, class from class, nation from nation, ideology from ideology, Gentile from Jew. What is true of the world of outer nature is true of human nature. In every individual there is a tension; each one of us is a walking civil war, torn between the desire for good and the desire for evil; we hate our sins and love them at one and the same time. According to both Greek and Jewish thought in the time of Paul, this disharmony extends even to the heavenly places. A cosmic battle is raging between the powers of evil and the powers of good, between God and the demons. Worst of all, there is disharmony between God and human beings. Men and women, who were meant to be in fellowship with God, are estranged from him.

So, in this world without Christ, there is nothing but disunity. That disunity is not God's purpose, but it can become a unity only when all things are united in Christ. As E. F. Scott has it in his commentary: 'The innumerable broken strands were to be brought together in Christ, knotted again into one, as they had been in the beginning.' The central thought of Ephesians is the realization of the disunity in the universe and the conviction that it can become unity only when everything is united in Christ.

The Origin of Paul's Thought

How did Paul arrive at this great conception of the unity of all things in Jesus Christ? Most probably, he came to it in two ways. It is surely the inevitable outcome of his conviction, stated so vividly in Colossians, that Christ is all-sufficient. But it may well be that there was something else which moved Paul's mind in this direction. He was a Roman citizen and proud of it. In his journeys, Paul had seen a great deal of the Roman Empire, and now he was in Rome, the imperial city. In the Roman Empire, a new unity had come to the world. The *pax Romana*, the Roman peace, was a very real thing. Kingdoms and states and countries, which had struggled and been at war with each other, were gathered into a new unity in the empire which was Rome. It may well be that, in his imprisonment, Paul saw with new eyes how all this unity centred in Rome; and it may well have seemed to him a symbol of how all things must centre in Christ, if a disunited nature and world and humanity were ever to be gathered into a unity. Surely, far from being a conception that was beyond his thinking, all Paul's thinking and experience would lead him precisely to that.

The Function of the Church

It is in the first three chapters of the letter that Paul deals with this conception of the unity in Christ. In the last three chapters, he has much to say about the place of the Church in God's plan to bring about that unity. It is here that Paul produces one of his greatest phrases. The Church is the *body of Christ*. The Church is to be hands to do Christ's work, feet to run his errands, a mouth to speak for him. So, we have two lines of thought in Ephesians. First, Christ is God's instrument of reconciliation. Second, the Church is Christ's instrument of reconciliation. The Church must bring Christ to the world; and it is within the Church that all the middle walls of separation must be broken down. It is through the Church that the unity of all the discordant elements must be achieved. As the

New Testament scholar E. F. Scott has it: 'The Church stands for that purpose of worldwide reconciliation for which Christ appeared, and in all their intercourse with one another Christians must seek to realize this formative idea of the Church.'

Who but Paul?

This is the thought of Ephesians. As we have seen, there are some who, thinking of the vocabulary and the style and the thought of this letter, cannot believe that Paul wrote it. E. J. Goodspeed, the American scholar, has put forward an interesting – but unconvincing – theory. The probability is that it was in Ephesus about the year AD 90 that the letters of Paul were first collected and sent out to the Church at large. It is Goodspeed's theory that the person responsible for that collection, some disciple of Paul, wrote Ephesians as a kind of introduction to the whole collection. Surely that theory breaks down on one obvious fact. Any imitation is inferior to the original. But, far from being inferior, Ephesians might well be said to be the greatest of all the Pauline letters. If Paul did not write it himself, we have to suggest as its writer someone who was possibly greater than Paul. E. F. Scott very relevantly demands: 'Can we believe that in the Church of Paul's day there was an unknown teacher of this supreme excellence? The natural assumption is surely that an epistle so like the work of Paul at his best was written by no other man than by Paul himself.' No one ever had a greater vision of Christ than this. It sees in Christ the one centre in whom all the disunities of life are gathered into one. No one ever had a greater vision of the Church than this – a vision which sees in the Church God's instrument in that worldwide reconciliation. And we may well believe that no one other than Paul could rise to a vision like that.

The Destination of Ephesians

We must now return to the problem which earlier we left unsolved. If Ephesians was not written to Ephesus, to what church was it written?

The oldest suggestion is that it was written to *Laodicea*. In Colossians 4:16, Paul writes: 'And when this letter has been read among you, have it read also in the church of the Laodiceans; and see that you read also the letter from Laodicea.' That sentence makes certain that a letter had gone from Paul to the church at Laodicea. We possess no such letter among Paul's letters as they stand. Marcion was one of the first people to make a collection of Paul's letters, around the middle of the second century, and he actually calls Ephesians the Letter to the Laodiceans. So, from very early times, there must have been a feeling in the Church that Ephesians was actually sent in the first instance to Laodicea.

If we accept that interesting and attractive suggestion, we still have to explain how the letter lost its individual address to Laodicea and came to be connected with Ephesus. There could be two explanations.

It may be that, when Paul died, the church at Ephesus knew that the church at Laodicea possessed a wonderful letter from Paul, and wrote to Laodicea asking for a copy. A copy may have been made and sent off, omitting only the words *in Laodicea* in the first verse, and leaving a blank as the earliest manuscripts have a blank there. Almost thirty years later, the letters of Paul were collected for general publication. Laodicea was in a district which was notorious for earthquakes, and it may well have been that all its archives were destroyed and that therefore, when the collection was made, the only copy of the Letter to the Laodiceans was the one which survived in Ephesus. That letter may then have come to be known as the Letter to the Ephesians, because it was in Ephesus that the only surviving copy was held.

The second suggested explanation was put forward by Adolf von Harnack, the great German scholar. In later times, the church in Laodicea sadly fell from grace. In the book of Revelation, there is a letter to Laodicea which makes sad reading (Revelation 3:14–22). In that letter, the church of Laodicea is unsparingly condemned by the risen Christ, so much so that he says in that vivid phrase: 'I am about to spit you out of my mouth' (Revelation 3:16). Now, in the ancient world there was a custom called *damnatio memoriae*, the condemnation of a person's memory. An individual might have rendered great service to the state, for which the name of that person might occur in books, in the state registers, in inscriptions and on memorials. But, if such a person ended in some base act, something utterly dishonourable, the memory of that person was condemned. The person's name was erased from all books, obliterated from all inscriptions and chiselled out of all memorials. Harnack thinks it possible that the church of Laodicea underwent a *damnatio memoriae* so that the city's name was obliterated from the Christian records. If that were so, then the copies of the Letter to Laodicea would have no address at all; and, when the collection was made at Ephesus, the name of Ephesus might well have become attached to it.

The Circular Letter

Both these suggestions are possible; but still another suggestion is far more likely. We believe that *Ephesians was not in fact written to any one church, but was a circular letter to all Paul's Asian churches*. Let us look again at Colossians

4:16. He writes: 'And when this letter has been read among you, have it read also in the church of the Laodiceans; and see that you read also the letter from Laodicea.' Paul does not say that the Colossians must read the epistle *to* Laodicea; they must read the epistle *from* Laodicea. It is as if Paul said: 'There is a letter circulating; at the present moment it has reached Laodicea; when it is sent on to you from Laodicea, be sure to read it.' That sounds very much as if there was a letter circulating among the Asian churches – and we believe that letter was Ephesians.

The Essence of Paul's Message

If this is so, Ephesians is Paul's supreme letter. We have seen that Ephesians and Colossians are very close to each other. We believe that what happened was that Paul wrote Colossians to deal with a definite situation, an outbreak of heresy. In so doing, he stumbled on his great expression of the all-sufficiency of Christ. He said to himself: 'This is something that I must get across to everyone.' So, he took the material he had used in Colossians, removed all the local and temporary and controversial aspects, and wrote a new letter to tell everyone about the all-sufficient Christ. Ephesians, as we see it, is the one letter Paul sent to all the eastern churches to tell them that the destined unity of all people and of all things could never be found except in Christ, and to tell them of the supreme task of the Church – that of being Christ's instrument in the universal reconciliation of all men and women to one another and of their reconciliation to God. That is why Ephesians is the Queen of the Epistles.

EPHESIANS

In Ephesians, Paul's argument is very closely woven together. It often proceeds in long, complicated sentences which are difficult to unravel. If we are really to grasp his meaning, there are passages where it will be better to read the letter first in fairly long sections and then to break down these sections into shorter passages for detailed study.

THE PURPOSE OF GOD

Ephesians 1:1–14

> This is a letter from Paul, an apostle of Jesus Christ, through the will of God, to God's consecrated people who live in Ephesus and who are faithful in Jesus Christ. Grace be to you, and peace from God our Father and from the Lord Jesus Christ.
>
> Blessed be the God and Father of our Lord Jesus Christ, who has blessed us with all the spiritual blessings which are only to be found in heaven, even as he chose us in him before the foundation of the world, that we might be holy and blameless before him. He determined in his love before time began to adopt us to himself through Jesus Christ, in the good purpose of his will, so that all might praise the glory of the generous gift which he freely gave us in the Beloved. For it is in him that

we have a deliverance which cost his life; in him we
have received the forgiveness of sins, which only the
wealth of his grace could give, a grace which he gave
us in abundant supply, and which conferred on us all
wisdom and all sound sense. This happened because he
made known to us the once hidden, but now revealed,
secret of his will, for so it was his good pleasure to do.
This secret was a purpose which he formed in his own
mind before time began, so that the periods of time
should be controlled and administered until they reached
their full development, a development in which all
things, in heaven and upon earth, are gathered into one
in Jesus Christ. It was in Christ, in whom our portion in
this scheme was also assigned to us, that it was determined, by the decision of him who controls everything according to the purpose of his will, that we, who
were the first to set our hopes upon the coming of the
Anointed One of God, should become the means
whereby his glory should be praised. And it was in
Christ that it was determined that you, too, should
become the means whereby God's glory is praised, after
you had heard the word which brings the truth, the good
news of your salvation – that good news in which, after
you had come to believe, you were sealed with the Holy
Spirit, who had been promised to you, the Spirit who is
the foretaste and guarantee of all that one day we will
inherit, until we enter into that complete redemption
which brings complete possession.

GREETINGS TO GOD'S PEOPLE

Ephesians I:I—2

This is a letter from Paul, an apostle of Jesus Christ,
through the will of God, to God's consecrated people

who live in Ephesus and who are faithful in Jesus Christ.
Grace be to you, and peace from God our Father and
from the Lord Jesus Christ.

PAUL begins his letter with the only two claims to fame which
he possessed. (1) He is *an apostle of Christ*. When Paul said
that, there were three things in his mind. (a) He meant that he
belonged to Christ. His life was not his own to do with as he
liked; he was the possession of Jesus Christ, and he must
always live as Jesus Christ wanted him to live. (b) He meant
that he was sent out by Jesus Christ. The word *apostolos*
comes from the verb *apostellein*, which means *to send out*. It
can be used, for instance, of a naval task force sent out on an
expedition; it can be used of ambassadors sent out by their
native countries. It describes people who are sent out with
some special task to do. All through life, Christians see themselves as members of the task force of Christ. They are men
and women with a mission, the mission of serving Christ
within this world. (c) He meant that *any power he possessed
was a delegated power*. The Sanhedrin was the supreme court
of the Jews. In matters of religion, the Sanhedrin had authority
over every Jew throughout the world. When the Sanhedrin
came to a decision, that decision was given to an *apostolos*
to convey it to the persons whom it concerned and to see that
it was carried out. When such an *apostolos* went out, behind
him and in him lay the authority of the Sanhedrin, whose
representative he was. Christians are the representatives of
Christ within the world, but they are not left to carry out that
task in their own strength and power; the strength and power
of Jesus Christ are with them.

(2) Paul goes on to say that he is an apostle *through the
will of God*. The accent in his voice here is not that of pride
but of sheer amazement. To the very end, Paul was amazed

that God could have chosen someone like him to do his work.
In words from F. W. Faber's hymn:

> How Thou canst think so well of us,
>   And be the God Thou art,
> Is darkness to my intellect,
>   But sunshine to my heart.

Christians must never be filled with pride in any task that
God gives them to do; they must be filled with wonder that
God thought them worthy of a share in his work.

Paul goes on to address his letter to the people who live in
Ephesus and who are faithful in Jesus Christ. Christians are
people who always live a double life. Paul's friends were
people who lived *in Ephesus* and *in Christ*. Every Christian
has a human address and a divine address; and that is precisely
the secret of the Christian life. The novelist Alistair MacLean
tells of a lady in the western highlands of Scotland who lived
a hard life, yet one of perpetual serenity. When asked the
secret of it, she answered: 'My secret is to sail the seas, and
always to keep my heart in port.' Wherever Christians are,
they are still in Christ.

Paul begins with his usual greeting. 'Grace to you,' he
says, 'and peace.' Here are the two great words of the
Christian faith.

Grace has always two main ideas in it. The Greek word is
charis, which could mean *charm*. There must be a certain
loveliness in the Christian life. A Christianity which is un-
attractive is no real Christianity. Grace always describes a
gift, and a gift which it would have been impossible to gain
for ourselves, and which we never earned and in no way
deserved. Whenever we mention the word *grace*, we must
think of the sheer loveliness of the Christian life and the sheer
undeserved generosity of the heart of God.

When we think of the word *peace* in connection with the Christian life, we must be careful. In Greek, the word is *eirene*; but it translates the Hebrew word *shalom*. In the Bible, *peace* is never a purely negative word; it never describes simply the absence of trouble. *Shalom* means everything which makes for a person's highest good. Christian peace is something quite independent of outward circumstances. People might have easy lives, living in luxury and off the fat of the land; they might have the finest of houses and the biggest of bank balances, and yet not have peace; on the other hand, others might be starving in prison, or dying as martyrs, or living a life deprived of comfort, and be at perfect peace. The explanation is that there is only one source of peace in all the world, and that is doing the will of God. When we are doing something which we know we ought not to do or are evading something that we know we ought to do, there is always a haunting disquiet at the back of our minds; but, if we are doing something very difficult, even something we do not want to do, as long as we know that it is the right thing, there is a certain contentment in our hearts. 'In his will is our peace.'

CHOSEN BY GOD

Ephesians 1:3-4

> Blessed be the God and Father of our Lord Jesus Christ, who has blessed us with all the spiritual blessings which are only to be found in heaven, even as he chose us in him before the foundation of the world, that we might be holy and blameless before him.

In the Greek, the long passage from verses 3-14 is one sentence. It is so long and complicated because it represents not so much a reasoned statement as a lyrical song of praise.

Paul's mind goes on and on, not because he is thinking in logical stages, but because gift after gift and wonder after wonder from God pass before his eyes. To understand it, we must break it up and take it in short sections.

In this section, Paul is thinking of Christians as the chosen people of God, and his mind runs along three lines.

(1) He thinks of *the fact of God's choice*. Paul never thought of himself as having chosen to do God's work. He always thought of God as having chosen him. Jesus said to his disciples: 'You did not choose me but I chose you' (John 15:16). Here precisely lies the wonder. It would not be so wonderful that we should choose God; the wonder is that God should choose us.

(2) Paul thinks of *the generosity of God's choice*. God chose us to bless us with the blessings which are to be found only in heaven. There are certain things which we can discover for ourselves; but there are others which are beyond us. People can acquire certain skills, can reach certain positions, can amass a certain amount of this world's goods by their own means; but by themselves they can never achieve goodness or peace of mind. God chose us to give us those things which he alone can give.

(3) Paul thinks of *the purpose of God's choice*. God chose us that we should be *holy* and *blameless*. Here are two great words. *Holy* is the Greek word *hagios*, which always has in it the idea of *difference* and of *separation*. A temple is *holy* because it is different from other buildings; priests are *holy* because they are different from ordinary men and women; an animal to be sacrificed is *holy* because it is different from other animals; God is supremely *holy* because he is different from us; the Sabbath is *holy* because it is different from other days. So, God chose Christians that they should be *different* from other people.

Here is the challenge that the modern Church has been very slow to face. In the early Church, Christians never had any doubt that they must be different from the world; they, in fact, knew that they must be so different that the probability was that the world would kill them and the certainty was that the world would hate them. But the tendency in the modern Church has been to play down the difference between the Church and the world. We have, in effect, often said to people: 'As long as you live a decent, respectable life, it is quite all right to become a church member and to call yourself a Christian. You don't need to be so very different from other people.' In fact, Christians should be easily identifiable in the world.

It must always be remembered that this difference on which Christ insists is not one which takes us *out* of the world; it makes us different *within* the world. It should be possible to identify Christians in the school, the shop, the factory, the office, the hospital ward, everywhere. And the difference is that Christians behave not as any human laws compel them to, but as the law of Christ compels them to. Christian teachers are out to satisfy the regulations not of an education authority or a headteacher but of Christ; and that will almost certainly mean a very different attitude to the pupils under their charge. Christian workers are out to satisfy the regulations not of a trade union but of Jesus Christ; and that will certainly make them very different workers. Christian doctors will never regard a sick person as a case, but always as a person. Christian employers will be concerned with far more than the payment of minimum wages or the creation of minimum working conditions. It is the simple fact of the matter that if enough Christians became *hagios*, different, they would revolutionize society.

Blameless is the Greek word *amōmos*. Its interest lies in the fact that it is a sacrificial word. Under Jewish law, before an animal could be offered as a sacrifice, it had to be inspected; and, if any blemish was found, it had to be rejected as unfit for an offering to God. Only the best was fit to offer to God. *Amōmos* thinks of the whole person as an offering to God. It thinks of taking every part of our life, work, pleasure, sport, home life and personal relationships, and making them all fit to be offered to God. This word does not mean that Christians must be respectable; it means that they must be perfect. To say that Christians must be *amōmos* is to banish contentment with everything that is second best; it means that the Christian standard is nothing less than perfection.

THE PLAN OF GOD

Ephesians 1:5–6

> He determined in his love before time began to adopt us to himself through Jesus Christ, in the good purpose of his will, so that all might praise the glory of the generous gift which he freely gave us in the Beloved.

In this passage, Paul speaks to us of the plan of God. One of the pictures that he uses more than once to illustrate what God does for us is that of adoption (cf. Romans 8:23; Galatians 4:5). God adopted us into his family as his children.

In the ancient world, where Roman law prevailed, this would be an even more meaningful picture than it is to us. For there, the family was based on what was called the *patria potestas*, the father's power. A father had absolute power over his children as long as he and they lived. He could sell his children as slaves or even kill them. The Roman historian Dio Cassius tells us that 'the law of the Romans gives a father absolute authority over his son, and that for the son's whole life. It gives him authority, if he so chooses, to imprison him, to scourge him, to make him work on his estate as a slave in fetters, even to kill him. That right still continues to exist even if the son is old enough to play an active part in political affairs, even if he has been judged worthy to occupy the magistrate's office, and even if he is held in honour by all men.' It is quite true that, when a father was judging his son, he was supposed to call the adult male members of the family into consultation; but it was not necessary that he should do so.

There are actual instances of a father condemning a son to death. The Roman historian and politician Sallust (*The Catiline Conspiracy*, 39) tells how Aulus Fulvius joined the rebel Catiline. He was arrested on the journey and brought back. And his father ordered that he should be put to death. The father did this on his own private authority, giving as his reason that 'he had begotten him, not for Catiline against his country, but for his country, against Catiline'.

Under Roman law, children could not possess anything; and any inheritance willed to them, or any gifts given to them, became the property of their father. It did not matter how old a son was, or to what honours and responsibility he had risen; he was absolutely in his father's power.

In circumstances like that, it is obvious that adoption was a very serious step. It was, however, not uncommon, for children were often adopted to ensure that some family line should not die out. The ritual of adoption must have been very impressive. It was carried out by a symbolic sale in which copper and scales were used. Twice the biological father sold his son, and twice he symbolically bought him back; finally he sold him a third time, and at the third sale he did not buy him back. After this, the adopting father had to go to the *praetor*, one of the principal Roman magistrates, and plead the case for the adoption. Only after all this had been gone through was the adoption complete.

When the process had been completed, the adoption was indeed complete. The person who had been adopted had all the rights of a legitimate son in his new family and lost absolutely all rights in his old family. In the eyes of the law, he was a new person. So new was he that even all debts and obligations connected with his previous family were abolished as if they had never existed.

That is what Paul says that God has done for us. We were absolutely in the power of sin and of the world; God, through Jesus, took us out of that power into his; and that adoption wipes out the past and makes us new.

THE GIFTS OF GOD

Ephesians 1:7–8

> For it is in him that we have a deliverance which cost his life; in him we have received the forgiveness of sins, which only the wealth of his grace could give, a grace which he gave us in abundant supply, and which conferred on us all wisdom and all sound sense.

In this short section, we come face to face with three of the great concepts of the Christian faith.

(1) There is *deliverance*. The word used is *apolutrōsis*. It comes from the verb *lutroun*, which means to *ransom*. It is the word used for ransoming someone who is a prisoner of war or a slave; for freeing someone from the penalty of death; for God's deliverance of the children of Israel from their slavery in Egypt; for God's continual rescuing of his people in the time of their trouble. In every case, the concept is of

delivering individuals from a situation from which they were powerless to liberate themselves or from a penalty which they could never have paid.

So, first of all, Paul says that God delivered people from a situation from which they could never have delivered themselves. That is precisely what Christianity did for us. When Christianity came into this world, men and women were haunted by the sense of their own powerlessness. They knew the wrongness of the life which they were living and that they were powerless to do anything about it.

The writings of the Stoic philosopher Seneca are full of this kind of feeling of helpless frustration. Human beings, he said, were overwhelmingly conscious of their inefficiency in necessary things. He said of himself that he was a *homo non tolerabilis*, a man not to be tolerated. Human beings, he said with a kind of despair, love their vices and hate them at the same time. What they need, he cried, is a hand let down to lift them up. The greatest thinkers in the Gentile world knew that they were in the grip of something from which they were helpless to deliver themselves. They needed liberation.

It was just that liberation which Jesus Christ brought. It is still true that he can liberate people from helpless slavery to the things which both attract and disgust them. To put it at its simplest, Jesus can still make bad people good.

(2) There is *forgiveness*. The ancient world was obsessed by the sense of sin. It might well be said that the Old Testament is an expansion of the saying: 'it is only the person that sins who shall die' (Ezekiel 18:4). People were conscious of their own guilt and stood in terror of their god or gods. It is sometimes said that the Greeks had no sense of sin. Nothing could be further from the truth. 'Men', said the Greek poet Hesiod, 'delight their souls in cherishing that which is their

bane.' All the plays of Aeschylus are founded on one text: 'The doer shall suffer.' Once someone had done an evil thing, Nemesis was on that person's heels; and punishment followed sin as certainly as night followed day. As Shakespeare had it in *Richard III*:

> My conscience hath a thousand several tongues,
> And every tongue brings in a several tale,
> And every tale condemns me for a villain.

If there was one thing which everyone knew, it was the sense of sin and the dread of God. Jesus changed all that. He taught people not of the hate but of the love of God. Because Jesus came into the world, men and women, even in their sin, discovered God's love.

(3) There is *wisdom* and *sound sense*. The two words in Greek are *sophia* and *phronēsis*, and Christ brought both of them to us. This is very interesting. The Greeks wrote a great deal about these two words; anyone who had both was perfectly equipped for life.

Aristotle defined *sophia* as knowledge of the most precious things. Cicero defined it as knowledge of things both human and divine. *Sophia* was a thing of the searching intellect. *Sophia* was the answer to the eternal problems of life and death, God and the world, and time and eternity.

Aristotle defined *phronēsis* as the knowledge of human affairs and of the things in which planning is necessary. Plutarch, the Greek historian and philosopher, defined it as practical knowledge of the things which concern us. The Roman orator Cicero defined it as knowledge of the things which are to be sought and the things which are to be avoided. Plato defined it as the disposition of mind which enables us to judge what things are to be done and what things are not to be done. In other words, *phronēsis* is the sound sense which enables us to meet and to solve the practical problems of everyday life and living,

It is Paul's claim that Jesus brought us *sophia*, the intellectual knowledge which satisfies the mind, and *phronēsis*, the practical knowledge which enables us to handle the day-to-day problems of practical life and living. There is a certain completeness in the Christian character. There is a type of person who is at home in the study, who moves among theological and philosophical problems with an easy familiarity, and who is yet helpless and impractical in the ordinary everyday affairs of life. There is another kind of person who claims to be practical and who is so engaged with the business of living that there is no time to be concerned with the ultimate things. In the light of the gifts of God through Christ, both of these characters are imperfect. Christ brings to us the solution of the problems both of eternity and of the present time.

THE GOAL OF HISTORY

Ephesians 1:9–10

> This happened because he made known to us the once hidden, but now revealed, secret of his will, for so it was his good pleasure to do. The secret was a purpose which he formed in his own mind before time began, so that the periods of time should be controlled and administered until they reached their full development, a development in which all things, in heaven and upon earth, are gathered into one in Jesus Christ.

It is now that Paul is really getting to grips with his subject. He says, as the Authorized Version has it, that God has made known to us 'the mystery of his will'. The New Testament uses the word *mystery* in a special sense. It is not something mysterious in the sense that it is hard to understand. It is something which has long been kept secret and has now been revealed, but is still incomprehensible to the person who has not been initiated into its meaning.

Let us take an example. Suppose someone who knew nothing whatever about Christianity was brought into a communion service. To that person, it would be a complete mystery; he or she would not understand in the least what was going on. But to anyone who knows the story and the meaning of the Last Supper, the whole service has a meaning which is quite clear. So, in the New Testament sense, a mystery is something which is hidden to non-Christians but clear to Christians.

What, for Paul, was the mystery of the will of God? It was that the gospel was open to the Gentiles too. In Jesus, God has revealed that his love and care, his grace and mercy, are meant not only for the Jews but for the whole world.

Now Paul, in one sentence, introduces his great thought. Up until now, people had been living in a divided world. There was division between the animals and human beings. There was division between Jews and Gentiles, Greeks and barbarians. All over the world, there was strife and tension. Jesus came into the world to wipe out the divisions. That, for Paul, was the secret of God. It was God's purpose that all the many different strands and all the warring elements in this world should be gathered into one in Jesus Christ.

Here, we have another tremendous thought. Paul says that all history has been a working out of this process. He says that all through the ages there has been an arranging and an administering of things so that this day of unity should come. The word which Paul uses for this preparation is intensely interesting. It is *oikonomia*, which literally means *household management.* The *oikonomos* was the steward who saw to it that the family affairs ran smoothly.

It is the Christian conviction that history is the working out of the will of God. That is by no means what every historian or thinker has been able to see. In one of his epigrams, the Irish playwright and poet Oscar Wilde said: 'You give the criminal calendar of Europe to your children under the name of history.' The historian and poet Sir George Clark, in his inaugural lecture at Oxford, said: 'There is no secret and no plan in history to be discovered. I do not believe that any future consummation could make sense of all the irrationalities of preceding ages. If it could not explain them, still less could it justify them.' In the introduction to *A History of Europe*, H. A. L. Fisher writes: 'One intellectual excitement, however, has been denied to me. Men wiser and more learned than I have discovered in history a plot, a rhythm, a predetermined pattern. These harmonies are concealed from me. I can see only one emergency following another, as wave follows upon wave, only one great fact with respect to which, since it is unique, there can be no generalizations, only one safe rule for the historian: that he should recognize in the development of human destinies the play of the contingent and the unforeseen.' The French novelist and biographer André Maurois says: 'The universe is indifferent. Who created it? Why are we here on this puny mud-heap spinning in infinite space? I have not the slightest idea, and I am quite convinced that no one has the least idea.'

It so happens that we are living in an age in which many people have lost their faith in any purpose for this world. But it is the faith of Christians that in this world God's purpose is being worked out; and Paul's conviction is that it is God's purpose that one day all things and all people should be one family in Christ. As Paul sees it, that mystery was not even grasped until Jesus came, and now it is the great task of the Church to work out God's purpose of unity, revealed in Jesus Christ.

JEWS AND GENTILES

Ephesians 1:11–14

It was in Christ, in whom our portion in this scheme was also assigned to us, that it was determined, by the decision of him who controls everything according to the purpose of his will, that we, who were the first to set our hopes upon the coming of the Anointed One of God, should become the means whereby his glory should be praised. And it was in Christ that it was determined that you, too, should become the means whereby God's glory is praised, after you had heard the word which brings the truth, the good news of your salvation – that good news in which, after you had come to believe, you were sealed with the Holy Spirit, who had been promised to you, the Spirit who is the foretaste and guarantee of all that one day we will inherit, until we enter into that complete redemption which brings complete possession.

HERE is Paul's first example of the new unity which Christ brings. When he speaks of *us*, he means his own nation, the Jews; when he speaks of *you*, he means the Gentiles to whom he is writing; and when in the very last sentence he uses *we*, it is of Jews and Gentiles together that he is thinking.

First of all, Paul speaks of the Jews. They, too, had their portion assigned to them in the plan of God. They were the first to believe in the coming of the Anointed One of God. All through their history, they had dreamed of and expected the

Messiah. Their part in the scheme of things was to be the nation from whom God's chosen one should come.

Adam Smith, the famous eighteenth-century economist, argued that the whole pattern of life was founded on what he called *the division of labour*. He meant that life can only go on when each person has a job and does that job, and when the results of all the jobs are pooled and become the common stock. The shoemaker makes shoes; the baker makes bread; the tailor makes clothes; individuals have their own jobs, and they stick to their own job; and, when each one of them efficiently carries out that job, the total good of the whole community follows.

What is true of individuals is true also of nations. Each nation has its part in God's scheme of things. The Greeks taught what beauty of thought and form is. The Romans taught law and the science of government and administration. The Jews taught religion. The Jews were the people who had been prepared through history for the appearance of God's Messiah from among them.

That is not to say that God did not prepare other people too. All over the world, God had been preparing individuals and nations so that their minds would be ready to receive the message of Christianity when it came. But the great privilege of the Jewish nation was that they were the first to expect the coming of the Anointed One of God into the world.

Then Paul turns to the Gentiles. In their development, he sees two stages.

(1) They received the word; to them the Christian preachers brought the Christian message. That word was two things. First, it was the word of truth; it brought them the truth about God and about the world in which they lived and about themselves. Second, it was good news; it was the message of the love and of the grace of God.

(2) They were sealed with the Holy Spirit. In the ancient world – it is a custom still followed – when a sack, or a crate, or a package was despatched, it was sealed with a seal, in order to indicate from where it had come and to whom it belonged. The possession of the Holy Spirit is the seal which shows that a person belongs to God. The Holy Spirit both shows us God's will and enables us to do it.

Here, Paul says a great thing about the Holy Spirit. He calls the Holy Spirit, as the Authorized Version has it, *the earnest of our redemption*. The Greek word is *arrabōn*. The *arrabōn* was a regular feature of the Greek business world. It was a part of the purchase price of anything, a deposit paid in advance as a guarantee that the rest would in due course be paid. There are many Greek commercial documents still in existence in which the word occurs. A woman sells a cow and receives so many drachmae as *arrabōn*. Some dancing girls are engaged for a public entertainment and are paid so much in advance. What Paul is saying is that the experience of the Holy Spirit which we have in this world is a foretaste of the blessedness of heaven; and it is the guarantee that some day we will enter into full possession of the blessedness of God.

The highest experiences of Christian peace and joy which this world can afford are only faint foretastes of the joy into which we will one day enter. It is as if God had given us enough to whet our appetites for more and enough to make us certain that some day he will give us all.

THE MARKS OF THE CHURCH

Ephesians 1:15–23

It is because I have heard of your faith in Jesus Christ, and your love to all God's consecrated people, that I never cease to give thanks for you, as I remember you in my prayers. It is the aim of my prayers that the God of our Lord Jesus Christ, the glorious Father, may give you the Spirit of wisdom, the Spirit which brings you new revelation, as you come to know him more and more fully. It is the aim of my prayers that the eyes of your heart may be enlightened, so that you may know what hope his calling has brought to you, what wealth of glory there is in our inheritance among the saints, what surpassing greatness there is in his power to us who believe with a belief which was wrought by the might of his strength, that power which wrought in Christ to raise him from among the dead, and to set him at God's right hand in the heavenly places, above every rule and authority and power and lordship, above every dignity which is held in honour, not only in this age, but also in the age to come. God subjected all things to him, and he gave him as head above all to the Church, which is his body, the Church which is his complement on earth, the Church which belongs to him who is filling all things in all places.

THE supremely important part, the second great step in Paul's argument, lies at the very end of this passage; but there are certain things we must note in the verses which precede it.

Here, there is set out before us in a perfect summary the characteristics of a true church. Paul has heard of their faith in Christ and their love to all God's consecrated people. The two things which must characterize any true church are *loyalty to Christ* and *love to other people.*

There is a loyalty to Christ which does not result in love to others. The monks and the hermits had a loyalty to Christ which made them abandon the ordinary activities of life in order to live alone in the desert places. The heresy-hunters of the Spanish Inquisition and of many other periods of history had a loyalty to Christ which made them persecute those who thought differently from them. Before Jesus came, the Pharisees had a loyalty to God which made them contemptuous of those whom they thought less loyal than themselves.

True Christians love Christ and they also love their neighbours. More than that, they know that they cannot show their love to Christ in any other way than by showing their love to their neighbours. However orthodox a church is, however pure its theology, and however noble its worship and its liturgy, it is not a true church in the real sense of the term unless it is characterized by love for other people. There are churches which seldom make any public pronouncement which is not based on censorious criticism. They may be orthodox, but they are not Christian. The true Church is marked by a double love – love for Christ and love for others.

The New Zealand minister F. W. Boreham quotes a passage from Robert Buchanan's *Shadow of the Sword*, in which Buchanan describes the Chapel of Hate. 'It stood on a bleak and barren moor in Brittany a hundred years ago. It was in ruins; the walls were black and stained with the slime of centuries; around the crumbling altar nettles and rank weeds grew breast high; whilst black mists, charged with rain, brooded night and day about the gloomy scene. Over the doorway of the chapel, but half-obliterated, was its name. It was dedicated to Our Lady of Hate. "Hither," says Buchanan, "in hours of passion and pain, came men and women to cry curses on their enemies – the maiden on her false lover, the lover on his false mistress, the husband on his false wife – praying, one and all, that Our Lady of Hate might hearken, and that the hated one might die within the year."' And then the novelist adds: 'So bright and so deep had the gentle Christian light shone within their minds!'

A chapel of hate is a grim concept; and yet – are we always so very far away from it? We hate the liberals or the radicals; we hate the fundamentalists or the conservatives; we hate those whose theology is different from our own; we hate the Roman Catholic or the Protestant as the case may be. We make pronouncements which are characterized not by Christian charity but by a kind of condemning bitterness. We would do well to remember every now and then that love of Christ and love of our neighbours cannot exist without each other. Our tragedy is that it is so often true, as the great satirist Jonathan Swift once said, that 'We have just enough religion to make us hate, but not enough to make us love one another.'

PAUL'S PRAYER FOR THE CHURCH

Ephesians 1:15-23 (*contd*)

In this passage, we see what Paul asks for a church which he loves and which is doing well.

(1) He prays for the Spirit of wisdom. The word he uses for *wisdom* is *sophia*, and we have already seen that *sophia* is the wisdom of the deep things of God. He prays that the church may be led deeper and deeper into the knowledge of the eternal truths. If that is ever to happen, certain things are necessary.

(a) It is necessary that we should have a thinking people. The eighteenth-century writer and biographer James Boswell tells us that the playwright Oliver Goldsmith once said: 'As I take my shoes from the shoemaker, and my coat from the tailor, so I take my religion from the priest.' There are many who are like that; and yet religion is nothing unless it is a personal discovery. As Plato wrote long ago:

103

'The unexamined life is the life not worth living,' and the unexamined religion is the religion not worth having. It is an obligation for thinking people to think their way to God.

(b) It is necessary that we should have a teaching ministry. The seventeenth-century theologian William Chillingworth said: 'The Bible, and the Bible only, is the religion of Protestants.' That is true; but so often we would not think so. The preaching and explanation of Scripture from the pulpit is a first requirement of religious wakening.

(c) It is necessary that we should have a readjusted sense of proportion. It is one of the strange facts of church life that, in official church gatherings such as sessions and presbyteries and even General Assemblies, a great many hours might be given to the discussion of mundane problems of administration for every one hour given to the discussion of the eternal truths of God.

(2) Paul prays for a fuller revelation and a fuller knowledge of God. For Christians, growth in knowledge and in grace is essential. Anyone who follows a profession knows that it is a mistake to stop studying. Doctors never think that they have finished learning when they leave university. They know that week by week, and almost day by day, new techniques and treatments are being discovered; and, if they want to continue to be of service to those who are ill and in pain, they must keep up with those advances. It is the same with Christians. The Christian life could be described as getting to know God better every day. A friendship which does not grow closer with the years tends to vanish with the years. And it is the same with us and God.

(3) Paul prays for a new realization of the Christian hope. It is almost a characteristic of the age in which we live that it

is an age of despair. The novelist Thomas Hardy wrote in *Tess of the D'Urbervilles*: 'Sometimes I think that the worlds are like apples on our stubbard tree. Some of them splendid and some of them blighted.' Then comes the question: 'On which kind do we live – a splendid one or a blighted one?' And Tess's answer is: 'A blighted one.' Between the wars, the historian Sir Philip Gibbs wrote: 'If I smell poison gas in Edgware Road, I am not going to put on a gas mask or go to a gas-proof room. I am going out to take a good sniff of it, for I shall know that *the game is up.*' The writer H. G. Wells once wrote grimly: 'Man, who began in a cave behind a windbreak, will end in the disease-soaked ruins of a slum.' On every side, the voice of the pessimist sounds; it was never more necessary to sound the trumpet-call of Christian hope. If the Christian message is true, the world is on the way not to disintegration but to consummation.

(4) Paul prays for a new realization of the power of God. For Paul, the supreme proof of that power was the resurrection. It proved that God's purpose cannot be stopped by any human action. In a world which looks chaotic, it is good to be aware that God is still in control.

(5) Paul finishes by speaking of the conquest of Christ in a sphere which does not mean so much to us today. As the Authorized Version has it, God has raised Jesus Christ 'far above all principality, and power, and might, and dominion, and every name that is named'. In Paul's day, people strongly believed both in demons and in angels; and these words which Paul uses are the titles of different grades of angels. He is saying that there is not a being in heaven or on earth to whom Jesus Christ is not superior. In essence, Paul's prayer is that we should realize the greatness of the Saviour God has given to us.

THE BODY OF CHRIST

Ephesians 1:15–23 (*contd*)

WE come to the last two verses of this chapter, and in them Paul has one of the most adventurous and most uplifting thoughts that anyone has ever had. He calls the Church by its greatest title – *the body of Christ*.

In order to understand what Paul means, let us go back to the basic thought of his letter. As it stands, this world is a complete disunity. There is disunity between Jews and Gentiles, between Greeks and barbarians; there is disunity between different people within the same nation; there is disunity within every individual, for in each one of us the good struggles with the evil; there is disunity between human beings and the natural world; and, above all, there is disunity between human beings and God. It was Paul's argument that Jesus died to bring all the discordant elements in this universe into one, to wipe out the separations, to reconcile people to one another and to reconcile them to God. Jesus Christ was above all things God's instrument of reconciliation.

It was to bring all things and all people into one family that Christ died. But, clearly, that unity does not yet exist. Let us take a human analogy. Suppose a great doctor discovers a cure for cancer. Once that cure is found, it is there. But, before it can become available for everyone, it must be taken out to the world. Doctors and surgeons must know about it and be trained to use it. The cure is there, but one individual cannot take it out to all the world; other doctors must be trained to be the agents whereby it reaches all the world's sufferers. That is precisely what the Church is to Jesus Christ. It is in Jesus that all people and all nations can become one; but, before that can happen, they must know about Jesus Christ. And it is the task of the Church to bring that about.

Christ is the head; the Church is the body. The head must have a body through which it can work. The Church is quite literally hands to do Christ's work, feet to run his errands, a voice to speak his words.

In the very last phrase of the chapter, Paul has two tremendous thoughts. The Church, he says, is the essential element in the work of Christ. Just as the ideas of the mind cannot become effective without the work of the body, the tremendous glory which Christ brought to this world cannot be made effective without the work of the Church. Paul goes on to say that Jesus is bit by bit filling all things in all places; and that act of filling is being worked out by the Church. This is one of the most tremendous thoughts in all Christianity. It means nothing less than that God's plan for one world is in the hands of the Church.

An illustration perfectly sums up this great truth. There is a legend which tells how Jesus went back to heaven after his time on earth. Even in heaven, he bore upon him the marks of the cross. The angels were talking to him, and Gabriel said: 'Master, you must have suffered terribly for men and women down there.' 'I did,' said Jesus. 'And,' said Gabriel, 'do they all know about how you loved them and what you did for them?' 'Oh no,' said Jesus, 'not yet. Just now, only a few people in Palestine know.' 'What have you done,' said Gabriel, 'to let everyone know about it?' Jesus said: 'I have asked Peter and James and John and a few others to make it the business of their lives to tell others about me, and the others still others, and yet others, until the furthest person on the widest circle knows what I have done.' Gabriel looked very doubtful, for he knew well what poor stuff human beings were made of. 'Yes,' he said, 'but what if Peter and James and John grow tired? What if the people who come after them forget? What if, way down in the twenty-first century, people just don't tell others about you? Haven't you made any other plans?' And Jesus answered: 'I haven't made any other plans. *I'm counting on them.*' To say that the Church is the body means that Jesus is counting on us.

THE CHRISTLESS LIFE AND THE GRACE OF GOD

Ephesians 2:1–10

> When you were dead in your sins and trespasses, those sins and trespasses in which once you walked, living life in the way in which this present age of this world lives it, living life as the ruler of the power of the air dictates it, that spirit who now operates in the children of disobedience – and once all we too lived the same kind of life as these children of disobedience do, a life in which we were at the mercy of the desires of our lower nature, a life in which we followed the wishes of our lower nature and of our own designs, a life in which, as far as human nature goes, we deserved nothing but the wrath of God, as the others do. Although we were all like that, I say, God, because he is rich in mercy, and because of his great love with which he has loved us, made us alive in Christ Jesus, even when we were dead in trespasses (it is by grace you have been saved), and raised us up with Christ, and gave us a seat in the heavenly places with Christ, because of what Christ Jesus did for us. This he did so that in the age to come the surpassing riches of his grace in his kindness to us in Christ Jesus might be demonstrated. For it is by grace appropriated by faith that you have been saved. You had nothing to do with this. It was God's gift to you. It was not the result of works, for it was God's design that no one should be able to boast. For we are his work,

created in Christ Jesus for good works, works which
God prepared beforehand that we might walk in them.

In this passage, Paul's thought flows on regardless of the
rules of grammar; he begins sentences and never finishes
them; he begins with one construction, and half-way through
he glides into another. That is because this is far more a poetic
expression of the love of God than a careful theological
exposition. The song of the nightingale is not to be analysed
by the laws of musical composition. The lark sings for the
joy of singing. That is what Paul is doing here. He is pouring
out his heart, and the claims of grammar have to give way to
the wonder of grace.

LIFE WITHOUT CHRIST

Ephesians 2:1-3

When you were dead in your sins and trespasses, those
sins and trespasses in which once you walked, living
life in the way in which this present age of this world
lives it, living life as the ruler of the power of the air
dictates it, that spirit who now operates in the children
of disobedience – and once all we too lived the same
kind of life as these children of disobedience do, a life
in which we were at the mercy of the desires of our
lower nature, a life in which we followed the wishes of
our lower nature and of our own designs, a life in which,
as far as human nature goes, we deserved nothing but
the wrath of God, as the others do.

When Paul speaks of *you*, he is speaking of the Gentiles;
when he speaks of *us*, he is speaking of the Jews, his own
people. In this passage, he shows how terrible the Christless
life was for both Gentiles and Jews.

(1) He says that that life was lived in sins and trespasses. The words he uses are interesting. The word for *sin* is *hamartia*; and *hamartia* is a shooting word. It literally means a *miss*. Someone shoots an arrow at the target; the arrow misses; that is *hamartia*. Sin is the failure to hit the target of life. That is precisely why sin is so universal.

We commonly have a wrong idea of sin. We would readily agree that those who rob or commit murder are sinners; but, since most of us are respectable citizens, in our heart of hearts we think that sin does not have very much to do with us. We would probably rather resent being called hell-deserving sinners. But *hamartia* brings us face to face with what sin is, the failure to be what we ought to be and could be.

Is a man as good a husband as he might be? Does he try to make life easier for his wife? Does he inflict his moods on his family? Is a woman as good a wife as she might be? Does she really try to understand her husband's problems and worries? Are we as good parents as we might be? Do we discipline and train our children as we ought, or do we often leave it to someone else? As our children grow older, do we come nearer to them, or do they drift away until conversation is often difficult and we and they are practically strangers? Are we as good sons and daughters as we might be? Do we ever even try to say thank you for what has been done for us? Do we ever see the hurt look in our parents' eyes and know that we put it there? Do we do our work as conscientiously as we should? Is every working hour filled with our best work, and is every task done as well as we could possibly do it?

When we realize what sin is, we come to see that it is not something which theologians have invented. It is something which is found in every aspect of life. It is the failure in any sphere of life to be what we ought to be and could be.

The other word Paul uses, translated as *trespasses*, is *paraptōma*. This literally means *a slip* or *a fall*. It is used for someone losing the way and straying from the right road; it is used for failing to grasp and slipping away from the truth. Trespass is taking the wrong road when we could take the right one; it is missing the truth that we should have known. Therefore, it is the failure to reach the goal we ought to have reached.

Are we in life where we ought to be? Have we reached the goal of efficiency and skill that our gifts might have enabled us to reach? Have we reached the goal of service to others that we might have reached? Have we reached the goal of goodness to which we might have attained?

The central idea of sin is failure – failure to hit the target, failure to hold to the road, failure to make life what it was capable of becoming – and that definition includes every one of us.

DEATH IN LIFE

Ephesians 2:1-3 (*contd*)

PAUL speaks about people being *dead in sins*. What did he mean? Some have taken it to mean that without Christ we live in a state of sin which in the life to come produces the death of the soul. But Paul is not talking about the life to come; he is talking about this present life. There are three directions in which the effect of sin is deadly.

(1) *Sin kills innocence*. No one is precisely the same after sinning. The psychologists tell us that we never forget anything.

It may not be in our conscious memory, but everything we ever did or saw or heard is buried in our subconscious memories. The result is that sin leaves a permanent effect on us.

In George Du Maurier's novel *Trilby*, there is an example of that. For the first time in his life, Little Billee has taken part in a drunken binge and has himself been drunk. 'And when, after some forty-eight hours or so, he had quite slept off the fumes of that memorable Christmas debauch, he found that a sad thing had happened to him, and a strange! It was as though a tarnishing breath had swept over the reminiscent mirror of his mind and left a little film behind it, so that no past thing he wished to see therein was reflected with quite the same pristine clearness. As though the keen, quick, razor edge of his power to reach and re-evoke the by-gone charm and glamour and essence of things had been blunted and coarsened. As though the bloom of that special joy, the gift he had of recalling past emotions and sensations and situations, and making them actual once more by a mere effort of will, had been brushed away. And he never recovered the full use of that most precious faculty, the boon of youth and happy childhood, and which he had once possessed, without knowing it, in such singular and exceptional completeness.'

The experience of sin had left a kind of tarnishing film on his mind, and things could never be quite the same again. If we stain a garment or a carpet, we may send it to be cleaned, but it is never quite the same again. Sin does something to people: it kills innocence; and innocence, once lost, can never be recovered.

(2) *Sin kills ideals*. In the lives of so many, there is a kind of tragic process. At first, people regard some wrong thing with horror; the second stage comes when they are tempted into doing it, but even as they do it, they are still unhappy and ill at ease and very conscious that it is wrong; the third stage is when they have done the thing so often that they do it

without a qualm. Each sin makes the next sin easier. Wordsworth wrote in 'Intimations of Immortality':

> The youth, who daily from the east
> Must travel, still is Nature's priest,
>   And by the vision splendid
>   Is on his way attended;
> At length the man perceives it die away,
> And fade into the light of common day.

Sin is a kind of suicide, for it kills the ideals which make life worth while.

(3) In the end, *sin kills the will*. At first, people engage in some forbidden pleasure because they want to; in the end, they engage in it because they cannot help it. Once a thing becomes a habit, it is not far from being a necessity. When someone has allowed some habit, some indulgence, some forbidden practice to take control, that person becomes its slave. As the old saying has it, 'Sow an act and reap a habit; sow a habit and reap a character; sow a character and reap a destiny.'

There is a certain murderous power in sin. It kills innocence; sin may be forgiven, but its effect remains. As the early Christian theologian Origen had it, 'The scars remain.' Sin kills ideals; people begin to do without a qualm the thing which once they regarded with horror. Sin kills the will; it takes such a hold that people cannot break free.

THE MARKS OF THE CHRISTLESS LIFE

Ephesians 2:1–3 (*contd*)

IN this passage, Paul makes a kind of list of the characteristics of life without Christ.

(1) It is life lived in the way this present age lives it. That is to say, it is life lived on the world's standards and with the world's values. Christianity demands *forgiveness*, but the ancient writers said it was a sign of weakness to have the power to avenge oneself for injury and not to do so. Christianity demands *love* even to our enemies, but the Greek historian Plutarch said that the sign of a good person was being useful to friends and terrible to enemies. Christianity demands *service*, but, to take one example, the world cannot understand the missionary who goes away to some foreign land to teach in a school or work in a hospital for a quarter of the salary that might be earned in some secular service. The essence of the world's standard is that it sets self in the centre; the essence of the Christian standard is that it sets Christ and others in the centre. The essence of the worldly man or woman is, as someone has said, that he or she 'knows the price of everything and the value of nothing'. The world's motive is profit; the Christian's dynamic is the desire to serve.

(2) It is life lived under the dictates of the prince of the air. Here again, we are dealing with something which was very real in the days of Paul but which is not so real to us. The ancient world had a strong belief in demons. They believed that the air was so crowded with these demons that there was not room to insert a pinpoint between them. Pythagoras said: 'The whole air is full of Spirits.' The Jewish philosopher Philo said: 'There are spirits flying everywhere through the air.' 'The air is the house of the disembodied spirits.' These demons were not all bad, but many of them were. They were out to propagate evil, to frustrate the purposes of God and to ruin human souls. Those who were under their domination had taken sides against God.

(3) It is a life characterized by disobedience. God has many ways of revealing his will to men and women. He does so by conscience, the voice of the Holy Spirit speaking within us; he does so by giving to us the wisdom and the commandments of his book; he does so through the advice of good and godly individuals. But those who live Christless lives take their own way of things, even when they know what God's way is.

(4) It is a life which is at the mercy of desire. The word for desire is *epithumia*, which characteristically means desire for something that is wrong and forbidden. To succumb to that is inevitably to come to disaster.

One of the tragedies of the nineteenth century was the career of Oscar Wilde. He had a brilliant mind, and won the highest academic honours; he was a scintillating writer, and won the highest rewards in literature; he had all the charm in the world and was a man whose instinct it was to be kind; yet he fell to temptation and came to prison and disgrace. When he was suffering for his fall, he wrote his book *De Profundis*, and in it he said: 'The gods had given me almost everything. But I let myself be lured into long spells of senseless and sensual ease . . . Tired of being on the heights I deliberately went to the depths in search for new sensation. What the paradox was to me in the sphere of thought, perversity became to me in the sphere of passion. I grew careless of the lives of others. I took pleasure where it pleased me, and passed on. I forgot that every little action of the common day makes or unmakes character, and that therefore what one has done in the secret chamber, one has some day to cry aloud from the house-top. I ceased to be lord over myself. I was no longer the captain of my soul, and did not know it. I allowed pleasure to dominate me. I ended in horrible disgrace.'

Desire is a bad master, and to be at the mercy of desire is to be a slave. And desire is not simply a physical thing; it is the craving for anything that is forbidden.

(5) It is the life which follows what the Authorized Version calls the desires of our flesh. We must be careful to understand what Paul means by the sins of the flesh. He means far more than sexual sins. In Galatians 5:19–21, Paul lists the sins of the flesh. True, he starts with adultery and fornication, but he goes on to idolatry, hatred, wrath, strife, envyings, dissensions and heresies. The flesh is that part of our nature which gives sin a way in and a point of attack.

The meaning of 'the flesh' will vary from person to person. One person's weakness may be physical desire and the risk may be sexual sin; another's may be in spiritual things and the risk in pride; another's may be in earthly things and the risk unworthy ambition; another's sin may be loss of temper and the risk in envyings and conflict. All these are sins of the flesh. Let no one think that, through escaping the grosser sins of the body, the sins of the flesh have been avoided. The flesh is anything in us which gives sin its chance; it is human nature without God. To live according to the dictates of the flesh is simply to live in such a way that our lower nature, the worse part of us, dominates our lives.

(6) It is life which is deserving only of the wrath of God. Many people's lives are embittered because they feel that they have never had what their talents and their efforts deserve; but in the sight of God no one deserves anything but condemnation. It is only their love in Christ which has forgiven men and women who deserved nothing but punishment from him – those who had responded to that love by causing grief and who had broken his law.

THE WORK OF CHRIST

Ephesians 2:4–10

> Although we were all like that, I say, God, because he is rich in mercy, and because of his great love with which he has loved us, made us alive in Christ Jesus, even when we were dead in trespasses (it is by grace you have been saved), and raised us up with Christ, and gave us a seat in the heavenly places with Christ, because of what Christ Jesus did for us. This he did so that in the age to come the surpassing riches of his grace in his kindness to us in Christ Jesus might be demonstrated. For it is by grace appropriated by faith that you have been saved. You had nothing to do with this. It was God's gift to you. It was not the result of works, for it was God's design that no one should be able to boast. For we are his work, created in Christ Jesus for good works, works which God prepared beforehand that we might walk in them.

PAUL had begun by saying that, as we are, we are dead in sins and trespasses; now he says that God in his love and mercy has made us alive in Jesus Christ. What exactly did he mean by that? We saw that there were three things involved in being dead in sins and trespasses. Jesus has something to do about each of them.

(1) We saw that sin kills innocence. Not even Jesus can give back lost innocence, for not even Jesus can put back the clock; but what he can do is take away the sense of guilt which the lost innocence necessarily brings with it.

The first thing sin does is create a feeling of estrangement between us and God. Whenever people realize that they have sinned, they are weighed down by the feeling that they dare not approach God. When Isaiah received his vision of God, his first reaction was to say: 'Woe is me! I am lost, for I am a man of unclean lips, and I live among a people of unclean lips' (Isaiah 6:5). When Peter realized who Jesus was, his first reaction was: 'Go away from me, Lord, for I am a sinful man!' (Luke 5:8).

Jesus begins by taking that sense of estrangement away. He came to tell us that, no matter what we are like, the door is open to the presence of God. Suppose there was a son or daughter who did some shameful thing and then ran away, because there was no point in going home, because the door was bound to be shut. Then suppose someone came with the news that the door was still open and a welcome was waiting at home. What a difference that news would make! It was just that kind of news that Jesus brought. He came to take away the sense of estrangement and of guilt, by telling us that God wants us just as we are.

(2) We saw that sin killed the ideals by which people live. Jesus reawakens the ideal in our hearts.

The story is told of an engineer in a river ferryboat in America. His boat was old and he did not worry overmuch about it; the engines were grimy and ill-cared for. This engineer was completely converted to Christianity. The first thing he did was to go back to his ferryboat and polish his engines until every part of the machinery shone like a mirror. One of the regular passengers commented on the change. 'What have you been up to?' he asked the engineer. 'What set you cleaning and polishing these old engines of yours?' 'Sir,' answered the engineer, 'I've got a glory.' That is what Christ does for people. He gives them a glory.

It is told that, in the congregation in Edinburgh to which the Scottish minister and hymn-writer George Matheson came, there was an old woman who lived in a cellar in filthy conditions. After some months of Matheson's ministry, communion time came round. When the elder called at this old woman's cellar, he found that she had gone. He tracked her down. He found her in an attic room. She was very poor and there were no luxuries, but the attic was as light and airy and clean as the cellar had been dark and dismal and dirty. 'I see you've changed your house,' he said to her. 'Ay,' she said, 'I have. You canna hear George Matheson preach and live in a cellar.' The Christian message had rekindled the ideal.

As the old hymn 'Rescue the perishing' has it:

> Down in the human heart, crushed by the tempter,
> Feelings lie buried that grace can restore.

The grace of Jesus Christ rekindles the ideals which repeated falling into sin has extinguished. And by that very rekindling, life begins climbing again.

(3) Greater than anything else, Jesus Christ revives and restores the lost will. We saw that the deadly thing about sin was that it slowly but surely destroyed a person's will and that the indulgence which had begun as a pleasure became a necessity. Jesus re-creates the will.

That in fact is always what love does. The effect of a great love is always to cleanse. When people really and truly fall in love, their love compels them to goodness. They love the loved one so much that the love for their sins is broken.

That is what Christ does for us. When we love him, that love re-creates and restores our will towards goodness. As Charles Wesley's great hymn 'O for a thousand tongues to sing' has it:

> He breaks the power of cancelled sin,
> He sets the prisoner free.

THE WORK AND THE WORKS OF GRACE

Ephesians 2:4–10 (*contd*)

PAUL closes this passage with a great discussion and explanation of that paradox which always lies at the heart of his view of the gospel. That paradox has two aspects.

(1) Paul insists that it is by grace that we are saved. We have not earned salvation, nor could we have earned it. It is the gift of God, and our part is simply to accept it. Paul's point of view is undeniably true – and for two reasons.

(a) God is perfection; and, therefore, only perfection is good enough for him. Human beings by their very nature cannot bring perfection to God; and so, if we are ever to win our way to God, it must always be God who gives and we take from him.

(b) God is love; sin is therefore a crime, not against law, but against love. Now, it is possible to make atonement for a broken law, but it is impossible to make atonement for a broken heart; and sin is not so much breaking God's law as it is breaking God's heart. Let us take a crude and imperfect analogy. Suppose a motorist by careless driving kills a child. The driver is arrested, tried, found guilty and sentenced to a term of imprisonment and/or to a fine. After the fine has been paid and/or the term of imprisonment served, as far as the law is concerned, the whole matter is over. But it is very different in relation to the mother whose child was killed. The driver can never put things right with her by serving a term of imprisonment and paying a fine. The only thing which can restore that relationship with her is an act of free forgiveness on her part. That is the way we are to God. It is not against God's laws that we have sinned, it is against his heart. And therefore only an act of free forgiveness of the grace of God can put us back into the right relationship with him.

(2) That is to say that actions have nothing to do with earning salvation. It is neither right nor possible to leave the teaching of Paul here – and yet that is where it is so often left. Paul goes on to say that we are re-created by God for good actions. Here is the Pauline paradox. All the good works in the world cannot put us right with God; but there is something radically wrong with the Christianity that does not result in good deeds.

There is nothing mysterious about this. It is simply an inevitable law of love. If some fine person loves us, we know that we do not and cannot deserve that love. At the same time, we know with utter conviction that we must spend our lives *trying* to be worthy of it.

That is our relationship to God. Good works can never earn salvation; but there is something radically wrong if salvation does not produce good actions. It is not that our good deeds put God in our debt; rather that God's love lays on us the obligation to try throughout our lives to be worthy of it.

We know what God wants us to do; God has prepared long beforehand the kind of life he wants us to live, and has told us about it in his book and through his Son. We cannot earn God's love; but we can and must show how grateful we are for it, by seeking with our whole hearts to live the kind of life that will bring joy to God's heart.

BC AND AD

Ephesians 2:11–22

So then remember that once, as far as human descent goes, you were Gentiles; you were called the uncircumcision by those who laid claim to that circumcision which is a physical thing, and a thing produced by men's hands. Remember that at that time you had no hope of a Messiah; you were aliens from the society of Israel, and strangers from the covenants on which the promises were based; you had no hope; you were in the world without God. But, as things now are, because of what Christ Jesus has done, you who were once far off have been brought near, at the price of the blood of Christ. For it is he who is our peace; it is he who made both Jew and Gentile into one, and who broke down the middle wall of the barrier between, and destroyed the enmity by coming in the flesh, and wiped out the law of commandments with all its decrees. This he did that in himself he might make the two into one new man, by making peace between them, and that he might reconcile both to God in one body through the cross, after he had slain the enmity by what he did. So he came and preached peace to you who were afar off, and peace to them who were near, because, through him, we both have the right of entry into the presence of the Father, for we come in the one Spirit. So then you are no longer strangers and foreigners resident in a land that is not their own, but you are fellow citizens with God's con-secrated people and members of the family of God. It is on the foundation of the prophets and the apostles that you have been built up; and the cornerstone is Christ himself. All the building that is going on is being fitted together in him, and it will go on growing until it becomes a holy temple in the Lord, a temple into which you too are built as part, that you may become the dwelling place of God, through the work of the Spirit.

BEFORE CHRIST CAME

Ephesians 2:11–12

> So then remember that once, as far as human descent
> goes, you were Gentiles; you were called the un-
> circumcision by those who laid claim to that circum-
> cision which is a physical thing, and a thing produced
> by men's hands. Remember that at that time you had
> no hope of a Messiah; you were aliens from the society
> of Israel, and strangers from the covenants on which
> the promises were based; you had no hope; you were in
> the world without God.

PAUL speaks of the condition of the Gentiles before Christ
came. Paul was the apostle to the Gentiles, but he never forgot
the unique place of the Jews in the design and the revelation
of God. Here, he is drawing the contrast between the lives of
the Gentiles and of the Jews.

(1) The Gentiles were called the uncircumcision by those
who laid claim to that circumcision which is a physical
sign and something performed by human hands. This was
the first of the great divisions. The Jews had an immense
contempt for the Gentiles. They said that the Gentiles were
created by God to be fuel for the fires of hell, and that God
loved only Israel of all the nations that he had made. 'The
best of the serpents crush,' they said, 'the best of the
Gentiles kill.' It was not even lawful to give help to a Gentile
woman in childbirth, for that would be to bring another
Gentile into the world. The barrier between Jews and Gentiles
was absolute. If a Jew married a Gentile, the funeral of that
Jew was carried out. Such contact with a Gentile was the
equivalent of death; even going into the house of a Gentile
made a Jew unclean. Before Christ, the barriers were up; after
Christ, the barriers were down.

(2) The Gentiles had no hope of a Messiah. The Authorized Version has it that they were *without Christ*. That is a perfectly possible translation; but the word *Christos* is not primarily a proper name, although it has become one. It is an adjective meaning *the Anointed One*. Kings were anointed at their coronations; and thus *Christos*, the literal Greek translation of the Hebrew *Messiah*, came to mean the Anointed One of God, the expected King whom God would send into the world to vindicate his own people and to bring in the golden age. Even in the days of their most bitter struggle, the Jews never doubted that that Messiah would come. But the Gentiles had no such hope.

See the result of that difference. For the Jews, history was always going somewhere; no matter what the present was like, the future was glorious; the Jewish view of history was essentially optimistic. On the other hand, for the Gentiles, history was going nowhere. To the Stoics, history was cyclical. They believed that it went on for 3,000 years; then there was a conflagration in which the whole universe was consumed in flames; then the whole process began all over again, and the same events and the same people exactly repeated themselves. To the Gentiles, history was a progress to nowhere; to the Jews, history was a march to God. To the Gentiles, life was not worth living; to the Jews, it was the way to greater life. With the coming of Christ, the Gentiles entered into that new view of history in which people are always on the way to God.

HOPELESS AND HELPLESS

Ephesians 2:11-12 (*contd*)

(3) The Gentiles were aliens from the society of Israel. What does that mean? The name for the people of Israel was

ho hagios laos, the *holy* people. We have seen (in 1:3–4) that
the basic meaning of *hagios* is *different*. In what sense were
the people of Israel different from other peoples? In the
sense that their only king was God. Other nations might be
governed by democracy or aristocracy; Israel was a theocracy
– a people ruled by God. Their governor was God. After his
triumphs, the people came to Gideon and offered him the
throne of Israel. Gideon's answer was: 'I will not rule over
you, and my son will not rule over you; the Lord will rule
over you' (Judges 8:23). When the psalmist sang: 'I will extol
you, my God and King' (Psalm 145:1), he meant it literally.

To be an Israelite was to be a member of the society of
God; it was to have a citizenship which was divine. Clearly,
life was going to be completely different for any nation which
had a consciousness of destiny like that. It is told that when
Pericles, the greatest of the Athenians, was walking forward
to address the Athenian assembly, he used to say to himself:
'Pericles, remember that you are an Athenian and that you
talk to Athenians.' For a Jew, it was possible to say:
'Remember that you are a citizen of God, and that you speak
to the people of God.' There is no consciousness of greatness
in all the world like that.

(4) The Gentiles were strangers from the covenants on
which the promises were based. What does that mean? Israel
was supremely *the covenant people*. What does that mean?
The Jews believed that God had approached their nation with
a special offer. 'I will take you as my people, and I will be
your God' (Exodus 6:7). This covenant relationship involved
not only privilege but also obligation. It involved the keeping
of the law. Exodus 24:1–8 gives us a dramatic picture of how
the Jewish people accepted the covenant and its conditions:
'All the words that the Lord has spoken we will do' (Exodus
24:3, cf. 24:7).

If God's design had ever to be worked out, it must be worked out through a nation. God's choice of Israel was not favouritism, for it was choice not for special honour but for special responsibility. But it gave to the Jews the unique consciousness of being the people of God. Paul could not forget, because it was a fact of history, that the Jews were uniquely the instrument in God's hand.

(5) The Gentiles were without hope and without God. People often speak of the Greeks as being the sunniest people in history; but there was such a thing as the Greek melancholy. Underlying everything, there was a kind of essential despair.

Even as far back as Homer, that is so. In the *Iliad* (6:146–9), Glaucus and Diomede meet in single combat. Before they close in combat, Diomede wishes to know the lineage of Glaucus, and Glaucus replies: 'Why enquirest thou of my generation? Even as are the generations of leaves such are those likewise of men; the leaves that be the wind scattereth upon the earth, and the forest buddeth and putteth forth more again, when the season of spring is at hand; so of the generations of men one putteth forth and another ceaseth.' The Greeks could say, as our great hymn 'Immortal, invisible' has it:

> We blossom and flourish as leaves on the tree,
> And wither and perish –

but they could not triumphantly add:

> But nought changeth thee.

The Greek poet Theognis could write:

> I rejoice and disport me in my youth; long enough beneath the earth shall I lie, bereft of life, voiceless as a stone, and shall leave the sunlight which I loved; good man though I am, then shall I see nothing more.

Rejoice. O my soul, in thy youth; soon shall other men
be in life, and I shall be black earth in death.

No mortal is happy of all on whom the sun looks down.

In the *Homeric Hymns*, the assembly of Olympus is
charmed by the Muses who sing 'of the deathless gifts of the
gods and the sorrows of men, even all that they endure by
the will of the immortals, living heedless and helpless, nor
can they find a cure for death, nor a defence against old
age'.

In Sophocles, we find some of the loveliest and the saddest
lines in all history.

Youth's beauty fades, and manhood's glory fades.
Faith dies and unfaith blossoms as a flower;
Nor ever wilt thou find upon the open streets of men,
Or secret places of the heart's own love,
One wind blows true for ever.

It was true that the Gentiles were without hope because
they were without God. Israel had always had the radiant
hope in God which burned clearly and inextinguishably even
in the darkest and most terrible days; but in their hearts the
Gentiles knew only despair, before Christ came to give them
hope.

THE END OF BARRIERS

Ephesians 2:13–18

But, as things now are, because of what Christ Jesus
has done, you who were once far off have been brought
near, at the price of the blood of Christ. For it is he who
is our peace; it is he who made both Jew and Gentile

into one, and who broke down the middle wall of the barrier between, and destroyed the enmity by coming in the flesh, and wiped out the law of commandments with all its decrees. This he did that in himself he might make the two into one new man, by making peace between them, and that he might reconcile both to God in one body through the cross, after he had slain the enmity by what he did. So he came and preached peace to you who were afar off, and peace to them who were near, because, through him, we both have the right of entry into the presence of the Father, for we come in the one Spirit.

WE have already seen how the Jews hated and despised the Gentiles. Now Paul uses two pictures, which would be especially vivid to a Jew, to show how that hatred is killed and a new unity has come.

He says that those who were far off have been brought near. Isaiah had heard God say: 'Peace, peace, to the far and the near' (Isaiah 57:19). When the Rabbis spoke about accepting a convert into Judaism, they said that that person had been *brought near*. For instance, the Jewish Rabbinic writers tell how a Gentile woman came to Rabbi Eliezer. She confessed that she was a sinner and asked to be admitted to the Jewish faith. 'Rabbi,' she said, 'bring me near.' The Rabbi refused. The door was shut in her face; but now the door was open. Those who had been far from God were brought near, and the door was shut to no one.

Paul uses an even more vivid picture. He says that the middle wall of the barrier between has been torn down.

This is a picture from the Temple. The Temple consisted of a series of courts, each one a little higher than the one that went before, with the Temple itself in the inmost of the courts. First there was the Court of the Gentiles; then the Court of the Women; then the Court of the Israelites; then the Court of the Priests; and finally the Holy Place itself.

Only into the first of these courts could a Gentile come. Between it and the Court of the Women there was a wall, or rather a kind of screen of marble, beautifully made, and set into it at intervals were tablets which announced that if Gentiles proceeded any further they were liable to instant death.

Josephus, in his description of the Temple, says: 'When you went through these first cloisters unto the second court of the Temple, there was a partition made of stone all round, whose height was three cubits [four to five feet]. Its construction was very elegant; upon it stood pillars at equal distances from one another, declaring the law of purity, some in Greek and some in Roman letters that no foreigner should go within the sanctuary' (*The Jewish Wars*, 5:5:2). In another description, he says of the second court of the Temple: 'This was encom-passed by a stone wall for a partition, with an inscription which forbade any foreigner to go in under pain of death' (*Antiquities of the Jews*, 15:11:5). In 1871, one of these prohibiting tablets was actually discovered, and the inscription on it reads: 'Let no one of any other nation come within the fence and barrier around the Holy Place. Whosoever will be taken doing so will himself be responsible for the fact that his death will ensue.'

Paul knew that barrier well – for his arrest at Jerusalem, which led to his final imprisonment and death, was due to the fact that he had been wrongly accused of bringing Trophimus, an Ephesian Gentile, into the Temple beyond the barrier (Acts 21:28–9). So, the intervening wall with its barrier shut the Gentiles out from the presence of God.

THE EXCLUSIVENESS OF CHRISTLESS HUMAN NATURE

Ephesians 2:13-18 (contd)

IT is not to be thought that the Jews were the only people who put up the barriers and shut people out. The ancient world was full of barriers. There was a time, more than 400 years before this, when Greece was threatened with invasion by the Persians. It was the golden age of the city state. Greece was made up of famous cities – Athens, Thebes, Corinth and the rest – and it very nearly encountered disaster because the cities refused to co-operate to meet the common threat. 'The danger lay', the New Testament scholar T. R. Glover wrote, 'in every generation, in the same fact of single cities, furious for independence at all costs.'

Cicero, the Roman orator and statesman, could write much later: 'As the Greeks say, all men are divided into two classes – Greeks and barbarians.' The Greeks called anyone who could not speak Greek a barbarian; and they despised such people and put up the barriers against them. When Aristotle is discussing bestiality, he says: 'It is found most frequently among barbarians,' and by barbarians he simply meant non-Greeks. He talks of 'the remote tribes of barbarians belonging to the bestial class'. The most vital form of Greek religion was the mystery religions, and from many of them the barbarians were excluded. The Roman historian Livy writes: 'The Greeks wage a truceless war against people of other races, against barbarians.' Plato said that the barbarians are 'our enemies by nature'.

This problem of the barriers is by no means confined to the ancient world. The Methodist author Rita Snowden quotes two very relevant sayings. The Jesuit, Father Taylor of Boston, used to say: 'There is just enough room in the world for all the people in it, but there is no room for the fences which separate them.' The travel writer Sir Philip Gibbs, in *The Cross of Peace*, wrote: 'The problem of fences has grown to be one of the most acute that the world must face. Today there are all sorts of zig-zag and criss-crossing separating fences running through the races and people of the world. Modern progress has made the world a neighbourhood: God has given us the task of making it a brotherhood. In these days of dividing walls of race and class and creed we must shake the earth anew with the message of the all-inclusive Christ, in whom there is neither bond nor free, Jew nor Greek, Scythian nor barbarian, but all are one.'

The ancient world had its barriers. So, too, has our modern world. In any Christless society, there can be nothing but middle walls of partition.

THE UNITY IN CHRIST

Ephesians 2:13–18 (*contd*)

So, Paul goes on to say that in Christ these barriers are down. How did Christ destroy them?

(1) Paul says of Jesus: 'He is our peace.' What did he mean by that? Let us use a human analogy. Suppose two people have a difference and go to law about it; and the experts in the law draw up a document, which states the rights of the case, and ask the two conflicting parties to come together on the basis of that document. All the chances are that the division will remain unhealed, for peace is seldom made on the basis of a legal document. But suppose that someone whom both of these conflicting parties love comes and talks to them, there is every chance that peace will be made. When two parties are at variance, the surest

way to bring them together is through someone whom they both love.

That is what Christ does. *He* is our peace. It is in a shared love of him that people come to love each other. That peace is won at the price of his blood, for the great awakener of love is the cross. The sight of that cross awakens in the hearts of men and women of all nations love for Christ, and only when they all love Christ will they love each other. It is not through treaties and organizations that peace comes. There can be peace only in Jesus Christ.

(2) Paul says of Jesus that he wiped out the law of the commandments with all its decrees. What does that mean? The Jews believed that only by keeping the Jewish law was an individual considered good and able to achieve the friendship and fellowship of God. That law had been worked out into thousands and thousands of commandments and decrees. Hands had to be washed in a certain way; dishes had to be cleaned in a certain way; there was page after page about what could and could not be done on the Sabbath day; sacrifices had to be offered in connection with every occasion in life. The only people who fully kept the Jewish law were the Pharisees, and there were only 6,000 of them. A religion based on all kinds of rules and regulations, about sacred rituals and sacrifices and days, can never be a universal religion. But, as Paul said elsewhere, 'Christ is the end of the law' (Romans 10:4). Jesus ended legalism as a principle of religion.

In its place, he put love for God and love for other people. Jesus came to tell people that they cannot earn God's approval by simply keeping the ceremonial law, but must accept the forgiveness and fellowship which God in mercy freely offers them. A religion based on love can immediately become a universal religion.

Rita Snowden tells a story from the Second World War. In France, some soldiers with their sergeant brought the body of a dead comrade to a French cemetery to have him buried. The priest told them gently that he was bound to ask if their comrade had been a baptized member of the Roman Catholic Church. They said that they did not know. The priest said that he was very sorry but in that case he could not permit burial in his churchyard. So, the soldiers took their comrade sadly and buried him just outside the fence. The next day they came back to see that the grave was all right and to their astonishment could not find it. Search as they might, they could find no trace of the freshly dug soil. As they were about to leave in bewilderment, the priest came up. He told them that his heart had been troubled because of his refusal to allow their dead comrade to be buried in the churchyard; so, early in the morning, he had risen from his bed and with his own hands *had moved the fence* to include the body of the soldier who had died for France.

That is what love can do. The rules and the regulations put up the fence; but love moved it. Jesus removed the fences between individuals because he abolished all religion founded on rules and regulations and brought to everyone a religion whose foundation is love.

THE GIFTS OF THE UNITY OF CHRIST

Ephesians 2:13–18 (*contd*)

PAUL goes on to tell of the priceless gifts which come with the new unity in Christ.

(1) He made both Jew and Gentile into one new being.

In Greek, there are two words for new. There is *neos*, which is new simply in terms of time; a thing which is *neos* has come into existence recently, but there may well have been thousands of the same thing in existence before. A pencil produced in the factory this week is *neos*, but there already exist millions exactly like it. Then there is *kainos*, which means new in terms of *quality*. A thing which is *kainos* is new in the sense that it brings into the world a new quality in itself which did not exist before.

The word that Paul uses here is *kainos*; he says that Jesus brings together Jew and Gentile and from them both produces one new kind of person. This is very interesting and very significant; it is not that Jesus makes all the Jews into Gentiles, or all the Gentiles into Jews; he produces a new kind of person out of both, although they remain Gentiles and Jews. John Chrysostom, the famous preacher of the early Church, says that it is as if one should melt down a statue of silver and a statue of lead, and the two should come out gold.

The unity which Jesus achieves is not achieved by blotting out all racial characteristics; it is achieved by making all people of all nations into Christians. It is Jesus' purpose not that we should turn all people into one nation, but that there should be Christian Indians and Christian Africans whose unity lies in their Christianity. The oneness in Christ is in Christ and not in any external change.

(2) He reconciled both to God. The word Paul uses (*apokatallassein*) is the word used of bringing together friends who have been estranged. The work of Jesus is to show all men and women that God is their friend and that, therefore, they must be friends with each other. Reconciliation with God involves and necessitates reconciliation with one another.

(3) Through Jesus, both Jew and Gentile have the right of access to God. The word Paul uses for *access* is *prosagōgē*, and it is a word of many pictures. It is the word used of

bringing a sacrifice to God; it is the word used of bringing people into the presence of God so that they may be consecrated to his service; it is the word used for introducing a speaker or an ambassador into a national assembly; and above all it is the word used for introducing a person into the presence of a king. There was, in fact, at the Persian royal court an official called the *prosagōgeus* whose function was to introduce people who sought an audience with the king. It is a priceless privilege to have the right to go to some lovely and wise and saintly person at any time, to have the right to break in upon that person and to bring with us our troubles, our problems, our loneliness and our sorrow. That is exactly the right that Jesus gives us with regard to God.

The unity in Christ produces Christians whose Christianity is above all their local and racial differences; it produces people who are friends with each other because they are friends with God; it produces individuals who are one because they meet in the presence of God to whom they all have access.

THE FAMILY AND THE DWELLING PLACE OF GOD

Ephesians 2:19–22

So then you are no longer strangers and foreigners resident in a land that is not their own, but you are fellow citizens with God's consecrated people and members of the family of God. It is on the foundation of the prophets and the apostles that you have been built up; and the cornerstone is Christ himself. All the building that is going on is being fitted together in him, and it will go on growing until it becomes a holy temple in the Lord, a temple into which you too are built as part,

that you may become the dwelling place of God, through
the work of the Spirit.

PAUL uses two illuminating pictures. He says that the Gentiles
are no longer foreigners but full members of the family of
God.

Paul uses the word *xenos* for foreigner. In every Greek
city there were *xenoi*, and they did not lead an easy life. One
wrote home: 'It is better for you to be in your own homes,
whatever they may be like, than to be in a strange land.' The
foreigner was always regarded with suspicion and dislike.
Paul uses the word *paroikos* for *stranger*. The *paroikos* was
one step further on. A person described in this way was a
resident alien, someone who had taken up residence in a place
but who had never become a naturalized citizen; such people
paid a tax for the privilege of existing in a land which was
not their own. Both the *xenos* and the *paroikos* were always
on the fringe.

So, Paul says to the Gentiles: 'You are no longer among
God's people on sufferance. You are full members of the
family of God.' We may put this very simply; it is through
Jesus that we are at home with God.

Professor A. B. Davidson of New College, Edinburgh, tells
how he was in lodgings in a strange city. He was lonely. He
used to walk the streets in the evenings. Sometimes, through
an uncurtained window, he would see a family sitting round
the table or the fire in happy fellowship; then the curtain
would be drawn and he would feel shut out, and lonely in the
dark.

That is what cannot happen in the family of God. And that
is what should never happen in a church. Through Jesus, there
is a place for everyone in the family of God. People may put
up their barriers; churches may keep their communion tables

for their own members. God never does; it is the tragedy of the Church that it is so often more exclusive than God.

The second picture Paul uses is that of a building. He thinks of every church as a part of a great building and of every Christian as a stone built into the Church. Of the whole Church, the cornerstone is Christ; and the cornerstone is what holds everything together.

Paul thinks of this building going on and on, with each part of the building being fitted into Christ. Think of a great cathedral. Down among the foundations, there may be a Saxon crypt; on some of the doorways or the windows, there may be a Norman arch; one part may be Early English and another Decorated and another Gothic; some parts may have been added in our own day. There are all kinds of styles of architecture; but the building is a unity because through it all it has been used for the worship of God and for meeting with Jesus Christ.

That is what the Church should be like. Its unity comes not from organization, or ritual, or liturgy; it comes from Christ. *Ubi Christus, ibi ecclesia* – Where Christ is, there is the Church. The Church will achieve its unity only when it realizes that it exists not to propagate the point of view of any body of individuals, but to provide a home where the Spirit of Christ can dwell and where everyone who loves Christ can meet in that Spirit.

PRISON AND PRIVILEGES

Ephesians 3:1–13

To understand the connection of thought in this passage, it has to be noted that verses 2–13 are one long digression. The *for this cause* of verse 14 takes up again and resumes the *for this cause* of verse 1. Someone has spoken of Paul's habit of 'going off at a word'. A single word or idea can send his thoughts off at a tangent. When he speaks of himself as 'the prisoner of Christ', it makes him think of the universal love of God and of his part in bringing that love to the Gentiles. In verses 2–13, his thoughts go off on that track; and in verse 14 he comes back to what he meant to say when he began.

> It is for this cause that I Paul, the prisoner of Jesus Christ for the sake of you Gentiles – you must have heard of the share that God gave me in dispensing his grace to you, because God's secret was made known to me by direct revelation, as I have just been writing to you, and you can read again what I have just written, if you wish to know what I understand of the meaning of that secret which Christ brought, a secret which was not revealed to the sons of men in other generations as it has now been revealed to his consecrated apostles and prophets by the work of the Spirit. The secret is that the Gentiles are fellow heirs, fellow members of the same body, fellow sharers in the promise in Jesus Christ, through the good news of which I was made a servant through the free gift of the grace of God, which was given to me according to the working of his power. It is to me, who am less than the least of all God's consecrated people, that this privilege has been given – the privilege of preaching to the Gentiles the wealth of Christ, the full story of which no man can ever tell; the privileges of enlightening all men as to what is the meaning of that secret, which was hidden from all eternity, in the God who created all things. It was kept secret up until now in order that now the many-coloured wisdom of God should be made known through the Church to the rulers and powers in the heavenly places; and all this happened and will happen in accordance with the eternal design

which he purposed in Jesus Christ, through whom we have a free and confident approach to him through faith in him. I therefore pray that you will not lose heart because of my afflictions on your behalf, for these afflictions are your glory.

THE GREAT DISCOVERY

Ephesians 3:1-7

It is for this cause that I Paul, the prisoner of Jesus Christ for the sake of you Gentiles – you must have heard of the share that God gave me in dispensing his grace to you, because God's secret was made known to me by direct revelation, as I have just been writing to you, and you can read again what I have just written, if you wish to know what I understand of the meaning of that secret which Christ brought, a secret which was not revealed to the sons of men in other generations as it has now been revealed to his consecrated apostles and prophets by the work of the Spirit. The secret is that the Gentiles are fellow heirs, fellow members of the same body, fellow sharers in the promise in Jesus Christ, through the good news of which I was made a servant through the free gift of the grace of God, which was given to me according to the working of his power.

WHEN Paul wrote this letter, he was in prison in Rome awaiting trial before Nero, waiting for the Jewish prosecutors to come with their bleak faces and their malicious charges. In prison, Paul had certain privileges, for he was allowed to stay in a house which he himself had rented, and his friends were allowed access to him; but night and day he was still a prisoner chained to the wrist of the Roman soldier who was his guard and whose duty it was to see that Paul would never escape.

In these circumstances, Paul calls himself 'the prisoner of Christ'. Here is another vivid instance of the fact that Christians always have a double life and a double address. Any ordinary person would have said that Paul was the prisoner of the Roman government; and so he was. But Paul never thought of himself as the prisoner of Rome; he always thought of himself as the prisoner of Christ.

The point of view held by any individual can make all the difference in the world. There is a famous story of the days when Sir Christopher Wren was building St Paul's Cathedral. On one occasion, he was making a tour of the work in progress. He came to a man at work and asked him: 'What are you doing?' The man said: 'I am cutting this stone to a certain size and shape.' He came to a second man and asked him what he was doing. The man said: 'I am earning a living at my work.' He came to a third man at work and asked him what he was doing. The man paused for a moment, straightened himself and answered: 'I am helping Sir Christopher Wren build St Paul's Cathedral.'

If people are in prison for some great cause, they may either grumblingly regard themselves as being ill-used, or they may radiantly regard themselves as the standard-bearers of that great cause. In one case, prison is regarded as a penance; in the other, it is regarded as a privilege. When we are undergoing hardship, unpopularity or material loss for the sake of Christian principles, we may regard ourselves either as victims or as the champions of Christ. Paul is our example; he regarded himself not as the prisoner of Nero but as the prisoner of Christ.

In this section, Paul returns to the thought which is at the very heart of this letter. Into his life had come the revelation of the great secret of God. That secret was that the love and mercy and grace of God were meant not only for the Jews but for all people. When Paul had met Christ on the Damascus road, there had come to him a sudden flash of revelation. It was to the Gentiles that God had sent him 'to open their eyes so that they may turn from darkness to light and from the power of Satan to God, so that they may receive forgiveness of sins and a place among those who are sanctified by faith in me' (Acts 26:18).

This was a completely new discovery. The fundamental sin of the ancient world was contempt. The Jews despised the Gentiles as worthless in the sight of God. At worst, they existed only to be annihilated: 'For the nation and kingdom that will not serve you shall perish; those nations shall be utterly laid waste' (Isaiah 60:12). At best, they existed to be the slaves of Israel: 'The wealth of Egypt and the merchandise of Ethiopia, and the Sabeans, tall of stature, shall come over to you and be yours, they shall follow you; they shall come over in chains and bow down to you' (Isaiah 45:14).

To people who could think like that, it was incredible that the grace and the glory of God were for the Gentiles. The Greeks despised the barbarians – and, to the Greeks, all other nations were barbarians. As the Roman philosopher Celsus said when he was attacking the Christians: 'the barbarians may have some gift for discovering truth, but it takes a Greek to understand'.

But, in the ancient world, the barriers were complete. No one had ever dreamt that God's privileges were for all people. It was Paul who made that discovery. That is why he is so tremendously important – for, had there been no Paul, it is conceivable that there would have been no worldwide Christianity and that we would not be Christians today.

THE SELF-CONSCIOUSNESS OF PAUL

Ephesians 3:1–7 (*contd*)

WHEN Paul thought of this secret which had been revealed to him, he thought of himself in certain ways.

(1) He regarded himself as the recipient of a new revelation. Paul never thought of himself as having *discovered* the universal love of God; he thought of God having *revealed* it to him. There is a sense in which truth and beauty are always given by God.

It is told that once Sir Arthur Sullivan was at a performance of *HMS Pinafore*. When that lovely duet 'Ah! Leave me not to pine alone' had been sung, Sullivan turned to the friend sitting beside him and said: 'Did I really write that?'

One of the great examples of poetical music of words is Samuel Taylor Coleridge's 'Kubla Khan'. Coleridge fell asleep reading a book in which were the words: 'Here Kubla Khan commanded a palace to be built and a stately garden thereunto.' He dreamed the poem, and when he woke up the only thing he had to do was write it down.

When scientists make a great discovery, over and over again what happens is that they think and think, and experiment and experiment – and come to a dead end. Then quite suddenly, in a flash, the solution to the problem comes to them. It is given to them – by God.

Paul would never have claimed to be the first person to discover the universality of the love of God; he would have said that God told him the secret which had not been previously revealed to anyone.

(2) He regarded himself as the transmitter of grace. When Paul meets the leaders of the Church to talk over with them his mission to the Gentiles, he talks about the gospel of the

uncircumcision being committed to him and of 'the grace that had been given to me' (Galatians 2:9). When he writes to the Romans, he speaks of 'the grace given me by God' (Romans 15:15). Paul saw his task as that of being a channel of God's grace to men and women. It is one of the great facts of the Christian life that we have been given the precious things of Christianity in order to share them with others. It is one of the great warnings of the Christian life that if we keep them to ourselves we lose them.

(3) He regarded himself as having the dignity of service. Paul says that he was made a servant by the free gift of the grace of God. He thought of his service not as a tiresome duty but as a glorious privilege. It is often astonishingly difficult to persuade people to serve the Church. To teach for God, to sing for God, to administer affairs for God, to speak for God, to visit those in poverty and distress for God, to give of our time and our talent and our substance for God, should not be counted a duty to be dragged or coaxed out of us; it is a privilege which we should be glad to accept.

(4) Paul regarded himself as a sufferer for Christ. He did not expect the way of service to be easy; he did not expect the way of loyalty to be trouble-free. Unamuno, the great Spanish mystic, used to say: 'May God deny you peace, and give you glory.' In his book *The Significance of Jesus*, W. Russell Maltby said that Jesus promised his disciples three things: 'they would be entirely fearless, absurdly happy, and that they would get into trouble'. When the knights of chivalry came to the court of King Arthur and to the society of the Round Table, they came asking for dangers to face and dragons to conquer. To suffer for Christ is not a penalty; it is our glory, for it is to share in the sufferings of Christ himself and an opportunity to demonstrate the reality of our loyalty to him.

THE PRIVILEGE WHICH MAKES US HUMBLE

Ephesians 3:8–13

> It is to me, who am less than the least of all God's
> consecrated people, that this privilege has been given –
> the privilege of preaching to the Gentiles the wealth of
> Christ, the full story of which no man can ever tell; the
> privileges of enlightening all men as to what is the
> meaning of that secret, which was hidden from all
> eternity, in the God who created all things. It was kept
> secret up until now in order that now the many-coloured
> wisdom of God should be made known through the
> Church to the rulers and powers in the heavenly places;
> and all this happened and will happen in accordance
> with the eternal design which he purposed in Jesus
> Christ, through whom we have a free and confident
> approach to him through faith in him. I therefore pray
> that you will not lose heart because of my afflictions on
> your behalf, for these afflictions are your glory.

PAUL saw himself as a man who had been given a double
privilege. He had been given the privilege of discovering the
secret that it was God's will that the whole world should be
gathered into his love. And he had been given the privilege
of making this secret known to the Church and of being the
instrument by which God's grace went out to the Gentiles.
But that awareness of privilege did not make Paul proud; it
made him intensely humble. He was amazed that this great
privilege had been given to him who, as he saw it, was less
than the least of God's people.

If ever we are privileged to preach or to teach the message
of the love of God or to do anything for Jesus Christ, we
must always remember that our greatness lies not in ourselves
but in our task and in our message. Toscanini was one of the

greatest orchestral conductors in the world. Once, when he was talking to an orchestra as he was preparing to play one of Beethoven's symphonies with them, he said: 'Gentlemen, I am nothing; you are nothing; Beethoven is everything.' He knew that his duty was not to draw attention to himself or to his orchestra but to let Beethoven flow through their playing.

Leslie Weatherhead, the broadcaster and counsellor, tells of a talk he had with a schoolboy who had decided to enter the ministry of the Church. He asked him when he had come to his decision, and the boy said he had been moved to make it after a certain service in the school chapel. Weatherhead very naturally asked who the preacher had been, and the boy answered that he had no idea; he only knew that Jesus Christ had spoken to him that morning. That was true preaching.

The tragic fact is that there are so many who are more concerned with their own importance and influence than with the significance of Jesus Christ, and who are more concerned that they should be noticed than that Christ should be seen.

THE PLAN AND THE WISDOM OF GOD

Ephesians 3:8–13 (*contd*)

THERE are still other things in this passage which we must note.

(1) Paul reminds us that the gathering in of all people was part of the eternal purpose of God. That is something which we would do well to remember. Sometimes, the history of Christianity can be presented in such a way that it sounds as if the gospel went out to the Gentiles only because the Jews would not receive it. Paul here reminds us that the salvation of the Gentiles is not an afterthought for God; the bringing of the whole world into his love was part of God's eternal design.

(2) Paul uses a great word to describe the grace of God. He calls it *polupoikilos*, which means *many-coloured*. The idea in this word is that the grace of God will match up to any situation which life may bring to us. There is nothing by way of light or of dark, of sunshine or of shadow, for which it is not triumphantly adequate.

(3) Again, Paul returns to one of his favourite thoughts. In Jesus, we have a free approach to God. It sometimes happens that one of our friends knows some very distinguished person. We ourselves would never have any right to enter into that person's presence; but in our friend's company we have the right of entry. That is what Jesus does for us with God. In his presence, there is an open door to God's presence.

(4) Paul finishes with a prayer that his friends may not be discouraged by his imprisonment. Perhaps they might think that the preaching of the gospel to the Gentiles will be greatly hindered because the champion of the Gentiles is in prison. Paul reminds them that the sufferings which he is enduring are for their good.

PAUL'S EARNEST PRAYER

Ephesians 3:14–21

> It is for this cause that I bow my knees in prayer before the Father, of whose fatherhood all heavenly and earthly fatherhood is a copy, that, according to the wealth of his glory, he may grant to you to be strengthened in the inner man, so that Christ through faith may take up his permanent residence in your hearts. I pray that you may have your root and your foundation in love, so that, with all God's consecrated people, you may have the strength fully to grasp the meaning of the breadth and length and depth and height of Christ's love, and to

know the love of Christ which is beyond all knowledge, that you may be filled until you reach the fullness of God himself.

To him that is able to do exceeding abundantly, above all that we ask or think, according to the power which works in us, to him be glory in the Church and in Christ Jesus to all generations forever and ever. Amen.

THE GOD WHO IS FATHER

Ephesians 3:14–17

It is for this cause that I bow my knees in prayer before the Father, of whose fatherhood all heavenly and earthly fatherhood is a copy, that, according to the wealth of his glory, he may grant to you to be strengthened in the inner man, so that Christ through faith may take up his permanent residence in your hearts.

Iᴛ is here that Paul picks up again the sentence which he began in verse I and from which he was deflected. He begins with the words: *It is for this cause.* What is the cause which makes him pray? We are back again at the basic idea of the letter. Paul has painted his great picture of the Church. This world is a disintegrated chaos; there is division everywhere, between nation and nation, between individuals, and within a person's inner life. It is God's design that all the discordant elements should be brought into one in Jesus Christ. But that cannot be done unless the Church carries the message of Christ and of the love of God to everyone. That is what Paul is praying for. He is praying that the people within the Church may be such that the whole Church will be the body of Christ.

We must note the word used for Paul's attitude in prayer. 'I bow my knees', he says, 'in prayer to God.' That means

3:14-17 EPHESIANS

even more than that he *kneels*; it means that he *prostrates* himself. The ordinary Jewish attitude of prayer was standing, with the hands stretched out and the palms upwards. Paul's prayer for the Church is so intense that he casts himself face down before God in an agony of passionate request.

His prayer is to God the Father. It is interesting to note the different things which Paul says in this letter about God as Father, for from them we get a clearer idea of what was in his mind when he spoke of the fatherhood of God.

(1) God is the Father of Jesus (1:2-3,1:17, 6:23). It is not true to say that Jesus was the first person to call God *Father*. The Greeks called Zeus the father of gods and of the people; the Romans called their chief god Jupiter, which means *Deus pater*, God the Father. But there are two closely interrelated words which have a certain similarity and yet a wide difference in their meaning.

There is *paternity*. Paternity means fatherhood in the purely physical sense of the term. It can be used of a fatherhood in which the father never even sees the child.

On the other hand, there is *fatherhood*. Fatherhood describes the most intimate relationship of love and of fellowship and of care.

When the word *father* was used of God before Jesus came, it was used much more in the sense of paternity. It meant that the gods were responsible for the creation of men and women. There was in the word none of the love and intimacy which Jesus put into it. The centre of the Christian conception of God is that he is like Jesus, that he is as kind, as loving and as merciful as Jesus was. It was always in terms of Jesus that Paul thought of God.

(2) God is the Father to whom we have access (2:18, 3:12).

The message of much of the Old Testament is that God was the person to whom access was forbidden. When

Manoah, who was to be the father of Samson, realized who his visitor had been, he said: 'We shall surely die, for we have seen God' (Judges 13:22). In the Jewish worship of the Temple, the Holy of Holies was held to be the dwelling place of God, and into it only the high priest might enter, and that only on one day of the year, the Day of Atonement.

The centre of Christian belief is the approachability of God. The folklorist and short-story writer H. L. Gee tells of a little boy whose father was promoted to the exalted rank of brigadier. When the little boy heard the news, he was silent for a moment, and then said: 'Do you think he will mind if I still call him daddy?' The essence of the Christian faith is unrestricted access to the presence of God.

(3) God is the Father of glory, the glorious Father (1:17). Here is the necessary other side of the matter. If we simply spoke about the accessibility of God, it would be easy to sentimentalize the love of God, and that is exactly what some people do. But the Christian faith rejoices in the wonder of the accessibility of God without ever forgetting his holiness and his glory. God welcomes sinners, but not if they want to trade on God's love in order to remain sinners. God is holy, and those who seek his friendship must be holy too.

(4) God is the Father of all (4:6). No individual, no Church, no nation has exclusive possession of God; that is the mistake which the Jews made. The fatherhood of God extends to all men and women, and that means that we must love and respect one another.

(5) God is the Father to whom thanks must be given (5:20). The fatherhood of God implies our debt to him. It is wrong to think of God as helping us only in the great moments of life. Because God's gifts come to us so regularly, we tend to forget that they are gifts. Christians should never forget that they

owe not only the salvation of their souls but also life and breath and all things to God.

(6) God is the pattern of all true fatherhood. That lays a tremendous responsibility on all human fathers. The writer G. K. Chesterton remembered his father only vaguely, but his memories were precious. He tells us that in his childhood he possessed a toy theatre in which all the characters were cut-outs in cardboard. One of them was a man with a golden key. He could never remember what the man with the golden key stood for, but in his own mind he always connected his father with him, a man with a golden key opening up all kinds of wonderful things.

We teach our children to call God 'father', and the only concept of fatherhood they can have is the one that we give them. Human fatherhood should be moulded on the fatherhood of God.

THE STRENGTHENING OF CHRIST

Ephesians 3:14–17 (*contd*)

PAUL prays that his people may be strengthened in their inner *being*. What did he mean? The inner *being* was a phrase by which the Greeks understood three things.

(1) There was human *reason*. It was Paul's prayer that Jesus Christ should strengthen the reason of his friends. He wanted them to be better able to discern between what was right and what was wrong. He wanted Christ to give them the wisdom which would keep life pure and safe.

(2) There was *conscience*. It was Paul's prayer that the conscience of his people should become increasingly sensitive. It is possible to disregard conscience for so long that in the end it becomes dulled. Paul prayed that

Jesus should keep our consciences sensitive and on the alert.

(3) There was the *will*. So often we know what is right, and mean to do it, but our will is not strong enough to back up our knowledge and to carry out our intentions. As the American poet John Drinkwater wrote in 'A Prayer':

> Grant us the will to fashion as we feel,
> Grant us the strength to labour as we know,
> Grant us the purpose, ribbed and edged with steel,
>   To strike the blow.
>
> Knowledge we ask not, knowledge Thou hast lent,
> But, Lord, the will – there lies our deepest need,
> Grant us the power to build, above the high intent,
>   The deed, the deed!

The inner being is the reason, the conscience, the will. The strengthening of the inner being comes when Christ takes up his permanent residence in an individual. The word Paul uses for Christ *dwelling* in our hearts is the Greek *katoikein*, which is the word used for permanent, as opposed to temporary, residence. Henry Lyte wrote, as one of the less familiar and now rarely sung verses of that great hymn 'Abide with me':

> Not a brief glance I beg, a passing word,
> But as thou dwell'st with thy disciples, Lord,
> Familiar, condescending, patient, free,
> Come, not to sojourn, but abide with me.

The secret of strength is the presence of Christ within our lives. Christ will gladly come into our lives – but he will never force his way in. He must await our invitation to bring us his strength.

THE INFINITE LOVE OF CHRIST

Ephesians 3:18–21

> I pray that you may have your root and your foundation in love, so that, with all God's consecrated people, you may have the strength fully to grasp the meaning of the breadth and length and depth and height of Christ's love, and to know the love of Christ which is beyond all knowledge, that you may be filled until you reach the fullness of God himself.
>
> To him that is able to do exceeding abundantly, above all that we ask or think, according to the power which works in us, to him be glory in the Church and in Christ Jesus to all generations forever and ever. Amen.

PAUL prays that Christians may be able to grasp the meaning of the breadth, depth, length and height of the love of Christ. It is as if Paul invited us to look at the universe – to the limitless sky above, to the limitless horizons on every side, to the depth of the earth and of the seas beneath us, and said: 'The love of Christ is as vast as that.'

It is unlikely that Paul had any more definite thought in his mind than the sheer vastness of the love of Christ. But many people have taken this picture and have read meanings, some of them very beautiful, into it. One ancient commentator sees the cross as the symbol of this love. The upper arm of the cross points up; the lower arm points down; and the crossing arms point out to the widest horizons. The fourth-century biblical scholar Jerome said that the love of Christ reaches up to include the holy angels, that it reaches down to include even the evil spirits in hell, that in its length it covers all who are striving on the upward way, and in its breadth it covers those who are wandering away from Christ.

If we want to work this out, we might say that in the *breadth* of its sweep, the love of Christ includes every individual of every kind in every age in every world; in the *length* to which it would go, the love of Christ accepted even the cross; in its *depth*, it descended to experience even death; in its *height*, he still loves us in heaven, where he lives always to make intercession for us (Hebrews 7:25). No one is outside the love of Christ; no place is beyond its reach.

Then Paul comes back again to the thought which dominates this letter. Where is that love to be experienced? We experience it *with all God's consecrated people*. That is to say, we find it in the fellowship of the Church. The founder of Methodism, John Wesley, had a saying which was true: 'God knows nothing of solitary religion.' 'No man', he said, 'ever went to heaven alone.' The Church may have its faults; church members may be very far from what they ought to be; but in the fellowship of the Church we find the love of God.

Paul ends with a hymn of praise to God, who can do for us more than we can dream of, and who does it for us in the Church and in Christ.

Once again, before we leave this chapter, let us think of Paul's glorious picture of the Church. This world is not what it was meant to be; it is torn apart by opposing forces and by hatred and bitter conflict. Nation is against nation, neighbour is against neighbour, class is against class. Within every individual, the fight rages between the evil and the good. It is God's design that all people and all nations should become one in Christ. To achieve this end, Christ needs the Church to go out and tell the world of his love and of his mercy. And the Church cannot do that until its members, joined together in fellowship, experience the limitless love of Christ.

EPHESIANS 4

WITH this chapter, the second part of the letter begins. In the first three chapters, Paul has dealt with the great and eternal truths of the Christian faith, and with the function of the Church in the plan of God. Now he begins to sketch what each member of the Church must be if the Church is to carry out its part in that plan.

Before we begin this chapter, let us again remind ourselves that the central thought of the letter is that Jesus has brought to a disunited world the way to unity. This way is through faith in him, and it is the Church's task to proclaim this message to all the world. And now Paul turns to the character that Christians must have if the Church is to fulfil the great task of being Christ's instrument of universal reconciliation between individuals, and between those same individuals and God within the world.

WORTHY OF OUR CALLING

Ephesians 4:1–10

> So then, I, the prisoner in the Lord, urge you to behave yourselves in a way that is worthy of the calling with which you are called. I urge you to behave with all humility, and gentleness, and patience. I urge you to bear with one another in love. I urge you eagerly to preserve that unity which the Holy Spirit can bring by binding things together in peace. There is one body and one Spirit, just as you have been called with one hope of your calling. There is one Lord, one faith, one baptism, one God and Father of all, who is above all, and through all, and in all. To each one of you grace has been given, as it has been measured out to you by

the free gift of Christ. Therefore Scripture says: 'He ascended into the height, and brought his captive band of prisoners, and gave gifts to men.' (When it says that 'he ascended', what else can it mean than that he also descended into the lower parts of the earth? He who descended is the same person as he who ascended above all the heavens, that he might fill all things with his presence.)

THE CHRISTIAN VIRTUES

Ephesians 4:1-3

So then, I, the prisoner in the Lord, urge you to behave yourselves in a way that is worthy of the calling with which you are called. I urge you to behave with all humility, and gentleness, and patience. I urge you to bear with one another in love. I urge you eagerly to preserve that unity which the Holy Spirit can bring by binding things together in peace.

WHEN we enter into any society, we take upon ourselves the obligation to live a certain kind of life; and if we fail in that obligation, we hinder the aims of our society and bring discredit on its name. Here, Paul paints the picture of the kind of life that people must live when they enter the fellowship of the Christian Church.

The first three verses shine like jewels. Here we have five of the great basic words of the Christian faith.

(1) First, and foremost, there is *humility*. The Greek is *tapeinophrosunē*, and this is actually a word which the Christian faith coined. In Greek, there is no word for humility which does not have some suggestion of meanness attached to it. Later, in the fourth century, Basil was to describe it as 'the gem casket of all the virtues'; but, before Christianity,

humility was not considered to be a virtue at all. The ancient world looked on humility as a thing to be despised.

The Greeks had an adjective for *humble*, which is closely connected with this noun – the adjective *tapeinos*. A word is always known by the company it keeps, and this word keeps disreputable company. It is used alongside the Greek adjectives which mean slavish (*andrapodōdēs*, *doulikos*, *douloprepēs*), ignoble (*agennēs*), of no repute (*adoxos*) and cringeing (*chamaizēlos*, which is the adjective which describes a plant that trails along the ground). In the days before Jesus, humility was looked on as a cowering, cringeing, servile, ignoble quality; and yet Christianity sets it in the very forefront of the virtues. Where does this Christian humility come from, and what does it involve?

(a) Christian humility comes from *self-knowledge*. The twelfth-century theologian Bernard of Clairvaux said of it: 'It is the virtue by which a man becomes conscious of his own unworthiness, in consequence of the truest knowledge of himself.'

To face oneself is the most humiliating thing in the world. Most of us see ourselves as playing great parts in life. There is a story about a man who, before he went to sleep at night, dreamt his waking dreams. He would see himself as the hero of some thrilling rescue from the sea or from the flames; he would see himself as an orator holding a vast audience spellbound; he would see himself walking to the wicket in a test match at Lord's cricket ground and scoring a century; he would see himself in some international football match dazzling the crowd with his skill; always he was the centre of the picture. Most of us are essentially like that. And true humility comes when we face ourselves and see our weakness, our selfishness, our failure in work and in personal relationships and in achievement.

(b) Christian humility comes from *setting life beside the life of Christ and in the light of the demands of God.*

God is perfection, and to satisfy perfection is impossible. As long as we measure ourselves by what is second best, we may come out of the comparison well. It is when we compare ourselves with perfection that we see our failure. A girl may consider herself a very fine pianist until she hears one of the world's outstanding performers. A man may think himself a good golfer until he sees one of the world's great professionals in action. Some people may consider themselves to be scholars until they pick up one of the books of the great old scholars of encyclopaedic knowledge. Others may think of themselves as fine preachers until they listen to one of the great inspirational preachers.

Self-satisfaction depends on the standard with which we compare ourselves. If we compare ourselves with our neighbours, we may well emerge very satisfactorily from the comparison. But the Christian standard is Jesus Christ and the demands of God's perfection – and against that standard there is no room for pride.

(c) There is another way of putting this. The Archbishop of Dublin, R. C. Trench, said that humility comes from the constant sense of our own *creatureliness*. We are in absolute dependence on God. As the hymn has it:

> 'Tis thou preservest me from death
>   And dangers every hour;
> I cannot draw another breath
>   Unless thou give me power.
>
> My health, my friends, and parents dear
>   To me by God are given;
> I have not any blessing here
>   But what is sent from heaven.

We are creatures, and for the creature there can be nothing but humility in the presence of the creator.

Christian humility is based on the sight of self, the vision of Christ, and the realization of God.

IN COMPLETE CONTROL

Ephesians 4:1–3 (*contd*)

(2) THE second of the great Christian virtues is what the Authorized Version calls *meekness* and what we have translated as *gentleness*. The Greek noun is *praotēs*, the adjective *praus*; and these are beyond translation by any single English word. *Praus* has two main lines of meanings.

(a) Aristotle, the great Greek thinker and teacher, has much to say about *praotēs*. It was his custom to define every virtue as the *mid-point between two extremes*. On one side there was excess of some quality, on the other defect; and in between there was exactly its right proportion. Aristotle defines *praotēs* as the mid-point between being too angry and never being angry at all. The person who is *praus* is the one who is always angry at the right time and never angry at the wrong time. To put that in another way, the person who is *praus* is the one who is stirred by indignation at the wrongs and the sufferings of others, but is never moved to anger by any personal wrongs and insults. So, the person who is (as in the Authorized Version) *meek* is the one who is always angry at the right time but never angry at the wrong time.

(b) There is another fact which will shed light on the meaning of this word. *Praus* is the Greek for an animal which has been trained and domesticated until it is completely under control. Therefore, the person who is *praus* is someone who has every instinct and every passion under perfect control. It would not be right to say that such a person is entirely self-controlled, for such self-control is beyond human power; but it would be right to say that such an individual is God-controlled.

Here, then, is the second great characteristic of true members of the Church. They are men and women who are so God-controlled that they are always angry at the right time but never angry at the wrong time.

PATIENCE THAT ENDURES

Ephesians 4:1–3 (contd)

(3) THE third great quality of a Christian is what the Authorized Version calls *long-suffering*. The Greek word is *makrothumia*. This word has two main directions of meaning.

(a) It describes the spirit which will never give in and which, because it endures to the end, will reap the reward. Its meaning can best be seen from the fact that a Jewish writer used it to describe what he called 'the Roman persistency which would never make peace under defeat'. In their great days, the Romans were unconquerable; they might lose a battle, they might even lose a campaign, but they could not conceive of losing a war. In the greatest disaster, it never occurred to them to admit defeat. Christian patience is the spirit which never admits defeat, which will not be broken by any misfortune or suffering, by any disappointment or discouragement, but which persists to the end.

(b) But *makrothumia* has an even more characteristic meaning than that. It is the characteristic Greek word for *patience with others*. John Chrysostom defined it as the spirit which has the power to take revenge but never does so. J. B. Lightfoot, the New Testament scholar, defined it as the spirit which refuses to retaliate. To take an imperfect analogy – it is often possible to see a puppy and a large dog together. The puppy yaps at the big dog, worries it, bites it, and all the time the big dog, which could put the puppy in its place with one snap of its teeth, bears the puppy's impertinence with a forbearing dignity. *Makrothumia* is the spirit which bears insult and injury without bitterness and without complaint. It is the spirit which can suffer unpleasant people with graciousness and fools without irritation.

The thing which best of all illustrates its meaning is that the New Testament repeatedly uses it of God. Paul asks unrepentant sinners if they despise the *patience* of God (Romans 2:4). Paul speaks of the perfect *patience* of Jesus to him (1 Timothy 1:16). Peter speaks of God's *patience* waiting in the days of Noah (1 Peter 3:20). He says that the forbearance of our Lord is our salvation (2 Peter 3:15). If God had been like us, he would long ago in sheer irritation have wiped the world out for its disobedience. Christians must have the patience towards their neighbours which God has shown to them.

CHRISTIAN LOVE

Ephesians 4:1–3 (*contd*)

(4) THE fourth great Christian quality is *love*. Christian love was something so new that the Christian writers had to invent a new word for it; or, at least, they had to employ a very unusual Greek word – *agape*.

In Greek, there are four words for *love*. There is *eros*, which is the love between the sexes and which involves sexual passion. There is *philia*, which is the warm affection which exists between those who are very near and very dear to each other. There is *storgē*, which is characteristically the word for family affection. And there is *agape*, which the Authorized Version sometimes translates as *love* and sometimes as *charity*.

The real meaning of *agape* is unconquerable benevolence. If we regard people with *agape*, it means that nothing that they can do will make us seek anything but their highest good. Even if they hurt us and insult us, we will never feel anything but kindness towards them. That quite clearly means that this Christian *love* is not an emotional thing. This *agape* is a thing not only of the emotions but also of the will. It is the ability to retain unconquerable goodwill towards the unlovely and the unlovable, towards those who do not love us, and even towards those whom we do not like. *Agape* is that quality of mind and heart which compels Christians never to feel any bitterness, never to feel any desire for revenge, but always to seek the highest good of absolutely everyone.

(5) These four great virtues of the Christian life – humility, gentleness, patience, love – lead to a fifth, *peace*. It is Paul's advice and urgent request that the people to whom he is writing should eagerly preserve 'the sacred oneness' which should characterize the true Church.

Peace may be defined as *right relationships one with another*. This oneness, this peace and these right relationships can be preserved only in one way. Every one of the four great Christian virtues depends on the obliteration of self. As long as self is at the centre of things, this oneness can never fully exist. In a society where self predominates, people cannot form anything but a disintegrated collection of individualistic and warring units. But when self dies and Christ springs to life within our hearts, then comes the peace, the oneness, which is the great hallmark of the true Church.

THE BASIS OF UNITY

Ephesians 4:4–6

> There is one body and one Spirit, just as you have been
> called with one hope of your calling. There is one Lord,
> one faith, one baptism, one God and Father of all, who
> is above all, and through all, and in all.

PAUL goes on to set down the basis on which Christian unity
is founded.

(1) There is one body. Christ is the head and the Church
is the body. No brain can work through a body which is split
into fragments. Unless there is a co-ordinated oneness in the
body, the plans and intentions of the head are frustrated. The
oneness of the Church is essential for the work of Christ.
That does not need to be a mechanical oneness of administration and of human organization; but it does need to be a
oneness founded on a common love of Christ and of every
part for the other.

(2) There is one Spirit. The word *pneuma* in Greek means
both *spirit* and *breath*; it is in fact the usual word for breath.
Unless the breath is in the body, the body is dead; and the
life-giving breath of the body of the Church is the Spirit of
Christ. There can be no Church without the Spirit; and there
can be no receiving of the Spirit without prayerful waiting.

(3) There is one hope in our calling. We are all proceeding
towards the same goal. This is the great secret of the unity of
Christians. Our methods, our organization, even some of our
beliefs may be different; but we are all striving towards the
one goal of a world redeemed in Christ.

(4) There is one Lord. The nearest approach to a creed
which the early Church possessed was the short sentence:
'Jesus Christ is Lord' (Philippians 2:11). As Paul saw it, it

was God's dream that there should come a day when everyone would make this confession. The word used for *Lord* is *kurios*. Its two usages in ordinary Greek show us something of what Paul meant. It was used for *master* as distinct from *servant* or *slave*; and it was the regular way of referring to the Roman emperor. Christians are joined together because they are all in the possession and in the service of the one Master and King.

(5) There is one faith. Paul did not mean that there is one *creed*. Very seldom indeed in the New Testament does the word *faith* mean a *creed*. By *faith*, the New Testament nearly always means the complete commitment of Christians to Jesus Christ. Paul means that all Christians are bound together because they have made a common act of complete surrender to the love of Jesus Christ. They may describe their act of surrender in different terms; but, however they describe it, that surrender is the one thing common to all of them.

(6) There is one baptism. In the early Church, baptism was usually adult baptism, because men and women were coming direct from the worship of other gods into the Christian faith. Therefore, above all, baptism was a public confession of faith. There was only one way for a Roman soldier to join the army: he had to take the oath that he would be true forever to his emperor. Similarly, there was only one way to enter the Christian Church – the way of public confession of Jesus Christ.

(7) There is one God. See what Paul says about the God in whom we believe.

He is the *Father* of all; in that phrase is enshrined the *love* of God. The greatest thing about the Christian God is not that he is king, nor that he is judge, but that he is Father. The Christian idea of God begins in love.

He is *above* all; in that phrase is enshrined the *control* of God. No matter what things may look like, God is in control. There may be floods; but 'The Lord sits enthroned over the flood' (Psalm 29:10).

He is *through* all; in that phrase is enshrined the *providence* of God. God did not create the world and set it going as we might wind up a clockwork toy and leave it to run down. God is all through his world, guiding, sustaining, loving.

He is *in* all; in that phrase is enshrined the *presence* of God in all life. It may be that Paul took the germ of this idea from the Stoics. The Stoics believed that God was a fire purer than any earthly fire; and they believed that what gave human beings life was that a spark of that fire which was God came and dwelt in their bodies. It was Paul's belief that in everything there is God.

It is the Christian belief that we live in a God-created, God-controlled, God-sustained, God-filled world.

THE GIFTS OF GRACE

Ephesians 4:7–10

> To each one of you grace has been given, as it has been measured out to you by the free gift of Christ. Therefore Scripture says: 'He ascended into the height, and brought his captive band of prisoners, and gave gifts to men.' (When it says that 'he ascended', what else can it mean than that he also descended into the lower parts of the earth? He who descended is the same person as he who ascended above all the heavens, that he might fill all things with his presence.)

PAUL turns to another aspect of his subject. He has been talking about the *qualities* of the members of Christ's Church;

164

now he is going to talk of their *functions* in the Church. He begins by laying down what was for him an essential truth – that every good thing that we have is the gift of the grace of Christ. As Harriet Auber's hymn has it:

> And every virtue we possess,
> And every victory won,
> And every thought of holiness,
> Are His alone.

To make his point about Christ the giver of gifts, Paul quotes, with a very significant difference, from Psalm 68:18. This psalm describes a king's conquering return. He ascends on high; that is to say, he climbs the steep road of Mount Zion into the streets of the holy city. He brings in his captive band of prisoners; that is to say, he marches through the streets with his prisoners in chains behind him to demonstrate his conquering power. Now comes the difference. The psalm speaks next about the conqueror *receiving* gifts. Paul changes it and says that he *gave* gifts to his people.

In the Old Testament, the conquering king *demanded and received* gifts; in the New Testament, the conqueror Christ *offers and gives* gifts. That is the essential difference between the two Testaments. In the Old Testament, a jealous God insists on tribute being paid; in the New Testament, a loving God pours out his love to men and women. That indeed is the good news.

Then, as so often, Paul's train of thought is diverted by a word. He has used the word *ascended*, and that makes him think of Jesus. And it makes him say a very wonderful thing. Jesus *descended* into this world when he entered it as a man; Jesus *ascended* from this world when he left it to return to his glory. Paul's great thought is that the Christ who ascended and the Christ who descended are one and the same person. What does that mean? It means that the Christ of glory is the same as the Jesus who trod this earth; still he loves all people; still he seeks out sinners; still he heals those who suffer; still he comforts the sorrowing; still he is the friend of outcast men and women. As the Scottish Paraphrase has it:

> Though now ascended up on high,
> He bends on earth a brother's eye;
> Partaker of the human name,
> He knows the frailty of our frame.

> Our fellow suff'rer yet retains
> A fellow-feeling of our pains;
> And still remembers in the skies
> His tears, His agonies and cries.

> In every pang that rends the heart
> The Man of sorrows has a part;
> He sympathizes with our grief,
> And to the suff'rer sends relief.

The ascended Christ is still the lover of human souls.

Still another thought strikes Paul. Jesus ascended up on high. But he did not ascend up on high to leave the world; he ascended up on high to fill the world with his presence. When Jesus was here on earth in human form, he could only be in one place at one time; he was under all the limitations of the body; but when he laid this body aside and returned to glory, he was set free from the limitations of the body and was able then to be everywhere in all the world through his Spirit. To Paul, the ascension of Jesus meant not a Christ-deserted but a Christ-filled world.

THE OFFICE-BEARERS OF THE CHURCH

Ephesians 4:11–13

> And he gave to the Church some as apostles, and some
> as prophets, and some as evangelists, and some as
> pastors and teachers. This he did that God's consecrated
> people should be fully equipped, that the work of service
> might go on, and that the body of Christ should be built
> up. And this is to go on until we all arrive at complete
> unity in faith in and knowledge of God, until we reach
> perfect manhood, until we reach a stature which can he
> measured by the fullness of Christ.

THERE is a special interest in this passage because it gives us
a picture of the organization and the administration of the
early Church. In the early Church, there were three kinds of
office-bearers. There were a few whose duties and authority
ran throughout the whole Church. There were many whose
ministry was not confined to one place but who carried out a
wandering ministry, going wherever the Spirit prompted them
to go. There were some whose ministry was a local ministry
confined to the one congregation and the one place.

(1) The *apostles* were those whose authority ran throughout the whole Church. The apostles included more than the
Twelve. Barnabas was an apostle (Acts 14:4, 14). James, the
brother of our Lord, was an apostle (1 Corinthians 15:7;
Galatians 1:19). Silvanus was an apostle (1 Thessalonians
2:7). Andronicus and Junias were apostles (Romans 16:7).

For an apostle, there were two great qualifications. First,
an apostle must have seen Jesus. When Paul is claiming his
own rights, faced by the opposition of Corinth, he demands:
'Am I not an apostle? Have I not seen Jesus our Lord?' (1
Corinthians 9:1). Second, an apostle had to be a witness of

the resurrection and of the risen Lord. When the eleven met to elect a successor to Judas the traitor, the one chosen had to be someone who had been with them throughout the earthly life of Jesus and had been a witness of the resurrection (Acts 1:21–2).

In a sense, the apostles were bound to die out, because before very long those who had actually seen Jesus and who had actually witnessed the resurrection would pass from this world. But, in another and still greater sense, the qualification remains. Anyone who would teach Christ must know Christ; and anyone who would bring the power of Christ to others must have experienced Christ's risen power.

(2) There were the *prophets*. The prophets did not so much *foretell* the future as *forthtell* the will of God. In forthtelling the will of God, they necessarily to some extent foretold the future, because they announced the consequences which would follow if people disobeyed that will.

The prophets were wanderers throughout the Church. Their message was held to be not the result of thought and study but the direct result of the Holy Spirit. They had no homes and no families and no means of support. They went from church to church proclaiming the will of God as God had told it to them.

Before long, the prophets vanished from the Church. There were three reasons why that happened. (a) In times of persecution, the prophets were the first to suffer; they had no means of concealment and were the first to die for the faith. (b) The prophets became a problem. As the Church grew, local organization developed. Each congregation began to grow into an organization which had its permanent minister and its local administration. Before long, the settled ministry began to resent the intrusion of these wandering prophets, who often disturbed their congregations. The inevitable result was that gradually the ministry of the prophets faded out. (c) The office of prophet was singularly liable to abuse. These prophetic wanderers had considerable prestige. Some of them abused their office and made it an excuse for living a very comfortable life at the expense of the congregations whom they visited. The earliest book of church administration is the *Didache*, *The Teaching of the Twelve Apostles*, which dates back to just after AD 100. In it, both the prestige and the suspicion of the prophets is clearly seen. The order for the sacrament is given, and the prayers to be used are set out; and then comes the instruction that prophets are to be allowed to celebrate the sacrament as they will. But there are certain other regulations. It is laid down that wandering prophets may stay one or two days with a congregation, but if they want to stay three days they are false prophets; it is laid down that any wandering prophet who, in a moment of alleged inspiration, demands money or a meal, is a false prophet.

(3) There were the *evangelists*. The evangelists, too, were wanderers. They corresponded to what we would call missionaries. Paul writes to Timothy: 'Do the work of an evangelist' (2 Timothy 4:5). They were the bringers of the good news. They did not have the prestige and authority of the apostles who had seen the Lord; they did not have the influence of the Spirit-inspired prophets; they were the ordinary missionaries of the Church who took the good news to a world which had never heard it.

(4) There were *the pastors and teachers*. It would seem that this double phrase describes one set of people. In one sense, they had the most important task in the whole Church. They were not wanderers but were settled and permanent in the work of one congregation. They had a triple function.

(a) They were *teachers*. In the early Church, there were few books. Printing was not to be invented for almost another

1,400 years. Every book had to be written by hand, and a book the size of the New Testament would cost as much as a whole year's wages for a working man. That meant that the story of Jesus had to be transmitted mainly by word of mouth. The story of Jesus was told long before it was written down; and these teachers had the tremendous responsibility of being the ones who preserved the memory of the gospel story. It was their function to know and to pass on the story of the life of Jesus.

(b) The people who came into the Church were coming straight from worship of Greek and Roman gods; they knew literally nothing about Christianity, except that Jesus Christ had taken hold of their hearts. Therefore these teachers had to reveal the full extent of the Christian faith to them. They had to explain the great doctrines of the Christian faith. It is to them that we owe the fact that the Christian faith remained pure and was not distorted as it was handed down.

(c) These teachers were also *pastors*. *Pastor* is the Latin word for a *shepherd*. At this time, the Christian Church was no more than a little island surrounded by the worship of other gods. The people who came into it were only one remove from their old way of life; they were in constant danger of lapsing into the old religions; and the duty of the pastor was to shepherd the flock and keep them safe.

The word is an ancient and an honourable one. As far back as the time of Homer, King Agamemnon was called the Shepherd of the People. Jesus had called himself the good shepherd (John 10:11, 10:14). The writer to the Hebrews called Jesus the great shepherd of the sheep (Hebrews 13:20). Peter called Jesus the shepherd of people's souls (1 Peter 2:25). He called him the chief shepherd (1 Peter 5:4). Jesus had commanded Peter to tend his sheep (John 21:16). Paul had warned the elders of Ephesus that they must guard the flock whom God had committed to their care (Acts 20:28). Peter had exhorted the elders to tend the flock of God (1 Peter 5:2).

The picture of the shepherd is indelibly written on the New Testament. The shepherd was the one who cared for the flock and led the sheep into safe places, the one who sought the sheep when they wandered away and, if need be, died to save them. The shepherd of the flock of God is the one whose heart bears God's people within it, who feeds them with the truth, who seeks them when they stray away, and who defends them from all that would hurt their faith. And the duty is laid on every Christian to be a shepherd to all other Christians.

THE AIM OF THE OFFICE-BEARERS

Ephesians 4:11-13 (*contd*)

AFTER Paul has named the different kinds of office-bearers within the Church, he goes on to speak of their aim and of what they must try to do.

Their aim is that the members of the Church should be fully equipped. The word Paul uses for *equipped* is interesting. It is *katartismon*, which comes from the verb *katartizein*. The word is used in surgery for setting a broken limb or for putting a joint back into its place. In politics, it is used for bringing together opposing factions so that government can go on. In the New Testament, it is used of mending nets (Mark 1:19) and of disciplining an offender until that person is fit to take up a place again within the fellowship of the Church (Galatians 6:1). The basic idea of the word is that of putting a thing into the condition in which it ought to be. It is the function of the office-bearers of the Church to see that the members of the Church are educated, guided, cared for and sought out when they go astray, in such a way that they become what they ought to be.

Their aim is that the work of service may go on. The word used for *service* is *diakonia*; and the main idea which lies behind this word is that of *practical service*. The office-bearers are not to be people who simply talk on matters of theology and of Church law; those who are appointed are in office to see that practical service of God's poor and lonely people goes on.

Their aim is to see to it that the body of Christ is built up. The work of the office-bearers is always construction, not destruction. Their aim is never to make trouble, but always to see that trouble does not rear its head; always to strengthen, and never to loosen, the fabric of the Church.

The office-bearers have even greater aims. Those already mentioned may be said to be their immediate aims; but beyond them they have still greater aims.

Their aim is that the members of the Church should arrive at perfect unity. They must never allow parties to form in the Church, or do anything which would cause differences in it. By principles and example, they must seek to draw the members of the Church into a closer unity every day.

Their aim is that the members of the Church should reach nothing less than perfection. The Church can never be content that its members should live decent, respectable lives; its aim must be that they should be examples of Christian perfection.

So, Paul ends with the greatest of all aims. The aim of the Church is that its members should reach a stature which can be measured by the fullness of Christ. The aim of the Church is nothing less than to produce men and women who have in them the reflection of Jesus Christ himself. In the nineteenth century, during the Crimean War, Florence Nightingale was passing one night down a hospital ward. She paused to bend over the bed of a sorely wounded soldier. As she looked down, the wounded youth looked up and said: 'You're Christ to me.' A saint has been defined as 'someone in whom Christ lives again'. That is what the true church member ought to be.

GROWING INTO CHRIST

Ephesians 4:14–16

> All this must be done so that we should no longer be infants in the faith, wave-tossed and blown hither and thither by every wind of teaching, by the clever trickery of men, by cunning cleverness designed to make us take a wandering way. Instead of that, it is all designed to make us cherish the truth in love, and to make us grow in all things into him who is the head – it is Christ I mean. It is from Christ that the whole body is fitted and united together, by means of all the joints which supply its needs, according as each part performs the share of the task allotted to it. It is from him that the body grows and builds itself up in love.

In every church, there are certain members who must be protected. There are those who are like children: they are dominated by a desire for novelty at the mercy of the latest fashion in religion. It is the lesson of history that popular fashions in religion come and go but the Church continues forever. The solid food of religion is always to be found within the Church.

In every church, there are certain people who have to be guarded against. Paul speaks of clever trickery; the word he uses (*kubeia*) means skill in manipulating the dice. There are always those who by ingenious arguments seek to lure people away from their faith. It is one of the characteristics of our age that people talk about religion more than they have done for many years; and Christians, especially young Christians, often have to meet the clever arguments of those who are against the Church and against God.

There is only one way to avoid being blown about by the latest religious fashion and to avoid being seduced by the convincing but wrong arguments of clever people, and that is by continual growth into Christ.

Paul uses another illustration. He says that a body is only healthy and efficient when every part is thoroughly co-ordinated. Paul says that the Church is like that; and the Church can be like that only when Christ is really the head and when every member is moving under his control, just as every part of a healthy body is obedient to the brain.

The only thing which can keep the individual Christian solid in the faith and secure against persuasive arguments that lead people astray, the only thing which can keep the Church healthy and efficient, is an intimate association with Jesus Christ, who is the head and the directing mind of the body.

THE THINGS WHICH MUST BE ABANDONED

Ephesians 4:17–24

> I say this and I solemnly lay it upon you in the Lord – you must no longer live the kind of life the Gentiles live, for their minds are concerned with empty things; their understandings are darkened; they are strangers from the life God gives, because of the ignorance that is in them and because of the petrifying of their hearts. They have come to a stage when they are past

feeling; and in their shameless wantonness they have abandoned themselves to every kind of unclean conduct in the insatiable lust of their desires. But that is not the way that you have learned Christ, if indeed you have really listened to him, and have been taught in him, as the true teaching in Jesus is. You must stop living in your former way of life. You must put off your old manhood, which is perishing, as deceitful desires are bound to make it do. You must be renewed in the spirit of your minds. You must put on the new self, created after God's pattern, in righteousness and in true holiness.

PAUL appeals to his converts to leave their old way of life and to turn to Christ's. In this passage, he picks out what he considers the essential characteristics of the life of non-Christians. Their lives are concerned with empty things which do not matter; their minds are darkened because of their ignorance. Then comes the all-important word: their hearts are *petrified*, turned to stone.

The word which Paul uses for the *petrifying* of their hearts is grim and terrible. It is *pōrōsis*. *Pōrōsis* comes from *pōrōs*, which originally meant a stone that was harder than marble. It came to have certain medical uses. It was used for the chalk stone which can form in the joints and completely paralyse action. It was used of the callus that forms where a bone has been broken and reset, a callus which is harder than the bone itself. Finally, the word came to mean the loss of all power of sensation; it described something which had become so hardened, so petrified that it had no power to feel at all.

That is what Paul says the life of those who have not discovered Christ is like. It has become so hardened that it has lost the power of feeling. In the 'Epistle to a Young Friend', Robert Burns wrote about sin:

> I waive the quantum o' the sin,
>   The hazard of concealing;
> But och! it hardens a' within,
>   And petrifies the feeling!

The terror of sin is its petrifying effect. The process of sin is quite discernible. No one becomes a great sinner all at once. At first, people regard sin with horror. When they sin, remorse and regret enter into their hearts. But, if people continue to sin, there comes a time when they lose all sensation and can do the most shameful things without any feeling at all. Their consciences have become petrified.

Paul uses two other terrible Greek words to describe the way of life of non-Christians. He says that they have abandoned themselves to every kind of unclean conduct in *the insatiable lust of their desires*, and that they have done so in their *shameless wantonness*.

The word for *shameless wantonness* is *aselgeia*. It is defined by Plato as 'impudence' and by another writer as 'preparedness for every pleasure'. It is defined by Basil the Great as 'a disposition of the soul incapable of bearing the pain of discipline'. The great characteristic of *aselgeia* is this: bad people usually try to hide their sin, but someone with *aselgeia* in the soul does not care how much public opinion is shocked as long as that person's personal desires are gratified. Sin can get such a grip of people that they are lost to decency and shame. They are like drug addicts who first take the drug in secret, but come to a stage when they openly beg for the drug on which they have become dependent. People can become slaves to alcohol to such an extent that they do not care who sees them drunk. People can let their sexual desires control them to such an extent that their only concern is to satisfy those desires.

Christless people do all this in the *insatiable lust of their desires*. The word is *pleonexia*, another terrible word, which the Greeks defined as 'arrogant greediness', as 'the accursed love of possessing', as 'the unlawful desire for the things which belong to others'. It has been defined as the spirit in which people are always ready to sacrifice others to their own desires. *Pleonexia* is the irresistible desire to have what we have no right to possess. It might find expression in the theft of material things; it might be evident in the spirit which tramples on other people to get its own way; it might lead to sexual sin.

In the world outside the Church, Paul saw three terrible things. He saw human hearts so turned to stone that they were not even aware that they were sinning; he saw people so dominated by sin that all sense of shame was lost and decency forgotten; he saw men and women so much at the mercy of their desires that they did not care whose life they injured and whose innocence they destroyed as long as these desires were satisfied. These are exactly the sins of the Christless world today, sins that can be seen invading life at every point and stalking the streets of every great city.

Paul urges his converts to have done with that kind of life. He uses a vivid form of language. He says: 'Put off your old way of life as you would put off an old suit of clothes; clothe yourself in a new way; put off your sins, and put on the righteousness and the holiness which God can give you.'

THINGS WHICH MUST BE BANISHED FROM LIFE

Ephesians 4:25–32

> So then strip yourselves of falsehood, and let each of
> you speak the truth with his neighbour, because we are

all members of the same body. Be angry – but be angry in such a way that your anger is not a sin. Do not let the sun set on your wrath, and do not give the devil any opportunity. Let him who was a thief steal no more; rather let him take to hard work, and to producing good with his hands, in order that he may be able to share with the man who is in need. Do not allow any foul word to issue from your mouth; but let your words be good, designed for necessary edification, that they may bring benefit to those who hear them. Do not grieve the Holy Spirit of God, with whom you are sealed until the day of your redemption comes. Let all bitterness, all outbreaks of passion, all long-lived anger, all loud talking, all insulting language be removed from you with all evil. Show yourselves kind to one another, merciful, forgiving one another, as God in Christ forgave you.

PAUL has just been saying that when people become Christians, they must put off their old life as they would put off a coat for which they have no further use. Here, he speaks of the things which must be banished from the Christian life.

(1) There must be no more falsehood. There is more than one kind of lie in this world.

There is the lie of speech, sometimes deliberate and sometimes almost unconscious. The great eighteenth-century man of letters, Dr Samuel Johnson, has an interesting piece of advice with regard to the bringing up of children. 'Accustom your children constantly to this [the telling of the truth]; if a thing happened at one window, and they, when relating it, say that it happened at another, do not let it pass, but instantly check them; you do not know where deviation from truth will end . . . It is more from carelessness about truth than from intentional lying, that there is so much falsehood in the world.' Truth demands a deliberate effort.

There is also the lie of silence, and maybe it is even more common. The French novelist André Maurois, in a memorable phrase, speaks of 'the menace of things unsaid'. It may be that in some discussion we, by our silence, give approval to some course of action which we know is wrong. It may be that we withhold warning or rebuke when we know quite well we should have given it.

Paul gives the reason for telling the truth. It is because we are all members of the same body. We can live in safety only because the senses and the nerves pass true messages to the brain. If they took to passing false messages – if, for instance, they told the brain that something was cool and touchable when in fact it was hot and burning – life would very soon come to an end. A body can function healthily only when each part of it passes true messages to the brain. If we are all bound into one body, that body can function properly only when we speak the truth.

(2) There must be anger in the Christian life, but it must be the right kind of anger. Bad temper and irritability are indefensible; but there is an anger without which the world would be a poorer place. The world would have lost much without the blazing anger of William Wilberforce against the slave trade of the British Empire or of Lord Shaftesbury against the working conditions of the nineteenth century.

There was a certain rugged bluntness about Dr Johnson. When he thought a thing was wrong, he said so with force. When he was about to publish the *Tour to the Hebrides*, the playwright and religious writer Hannah More asked him to tone down some of its harshness. She tells that his answer was that 'he would not cut off his claws, nor make his tiger a cat, to please anybody'. There is a place for the tiger in life; and when the tiger becomes a tabby cat, something is lost.

There were times when Jesus was terribly and majestically angry. He was angry when the scribes and Pharisees were watching to see if he would heal the man with the withered hand on the Sabbath day (Mark 3:5). It was not their criticism of himself at which he was angry; he was angry that their rigid orthodoxy wanted to impose unnecessary suffering on a fellow human being. He was angry when he made a whip and drove the money-changers and the sellers of animals for sacrifice from the Temple courts (John 2:13–17).

The nineteenth-century preacher F. W. Robertson of Brighton tells in one of his letters that he bit his lips until they bled when he met on the street a certain man whom he knew to be leading a pure young girl astray. John Wesley said: 'Give me a hundred men who fear nothing but God, and *who hate nothing but sin*, and who know nothing but Jesus Christ and him crucified, and I will shake the world.'

The anger which is selfish and uncontrolled is sinful and hurtful and must be banished from the Christian life. But the selfless anger which is disciplined into the service of Christ and of other people is one of the great dynamic forces of the world.

THINGS WHICH MUST BE BANISHED FROM LIFE

Ephesians 4:25–32 (*contd*)

(3) PAUL goes on to say that Christians must never let the sun set upon their anger. Plutarch, the Greek historian, tells us that the disciples of Pythagoras had a rule of their society that if, during the day, anger had made them speak insultingly to each other, before the sun set they shook hands and kissed each other and were reconciled. There was a

Jewish Rabbi whose prayer it was that he might never go to sleep with any bitter thought against a fellow human being within his mind.

Paul's advice is sound, because the longer we postpone putting right a quarrel, the less likely we are ever to sort things out. If there is trouble between us and anyone else, if there is trouble in a church or a fellowship or any society where people meet, the only way to deal with it is immediately. The longer it is left to flourish, the more bitter it will grow. If we have been in the wrong, we must pray to God to give us grace to admit it; and, even if we are in the right, we must pray to God to give us the graciousness which will enable us to take the first step to put matters right.

Along with this phrase, Paul puts another command. The Greek can equally well mean two things. It can mean: 'Don't give the devil his opportunity.' An unhealed division is a magnificent opportunity for the devil to sow disagreement. There have been many occasions when a church has been torn into factions because two people quarrelled and let the sun set upon their anger. But this phrase can have another meaning. The word for *devil* in Greek is *diabolos*; but *diabolos* is also the normal Greek for a *slanderer*. Martin Luther, for instance, took this to mean: 'Give the slanderer no place in your life.' It may well be that this is the true meaning of what Paul wants to say. No one in this world can do more damage than the slanderous gossip. As Samuel Taylor Coleridge wrote in 'Christabel':

> Alas! they had been friends in youth;
> But whispering tongues can poison truth.

There are reputations murdered through gossip every day; and when we see a tale-teller coming, we would do well to shut the door in that person's face.

(4) Thieves must become honest workers. This was necessary advice, for in the ancient world stealing was rampant. It was very common in two places – at the docks and above all in the public baths. The public baths were the private clubs of the time; and stealing the belongings of the bathers was one of the most common crimes in any Greek city.

The interesting thing about this saying is the reason Paul gives for being an honest worker. He does not say: 'Become an honest worker so that you may support yourself.' He says: 'Become an honest worker so that you may have something to give away to those who are poorer than yourself.' Here is a new idea and a new ideal – that of working in order to give away.

The journalist and theatre critic James Agate tells of a letter from Arnold Bennett, the famous novelist, to a less fortunate writer. Bennett was an ambitious and in many ways a worldly man; but, in this letter to a fellow writer whom he hardly knew, he says: 'I have just been looking at my bankbook; and I find that I have a hundred pounds which I don't need; I am sending you a cheque herewith for that amount.'

In modern society, not many of us have a great deal to give away; but we do well to remember that the Christian ideal is that we work not to accumulate things but to be able, if need be, to give them away.

(5) Paul forbids all foul-mouthed speaking, and then goes on to put the same thing positively. The Christian should be characterized by words which help others. As James Moffatt's translation has it, Eliphaz the Temanite paid Job a tremendous compliment. 'Your words', he said, 'have kept men on their feet' (Job 4:4). Such are the words that every Christian ought to speak.

(6) Paul urges us not to grieve the Holy Spirit. The Holy Spirit is the guide of life. When we act against the counsel of

our parents when we are young, we hurt them. Similarly, to act against the guidance of the Holy Spirit is to grieve the Spirit and to hurt the heart of God, the Father, who, through the Spirit, sent his word to us.

THINGS WHICH MUST BE BANISHED FROM LIFE

Ephesians 4:25–32 (*contd*)

PAUL ends this chapter with a list of things which must go from life.

(1) There is *bitterness* (*pikria*). The Greeks defined this word as *long-standing resentment*, the spirit which refuses to be reconciled. So many of us have a way of nursing our anger to keep it warm, of brooding over the insults and the injuries which we have received. As Christians, we all might well pray that God would teach us how to forget.

(2) There are *outbreaks of passion* (*thumos*) and *long-lived anger* (*orgē*). The Greeks defined *thumos* as the kind of anger which is like the flame which comes from straw; it quickly blazes up and just as quickly subsides. On the other hand, they described *orgē* as anger which has become habitual. To Christians, the burst of temper and the long-lived anger are both forbidden.

(3) There is *loud talking* and *insulting language*. A certain famous preacher tells how his wife used to advise him: 'In the pulpit, keep your voice down.' Whenever, in any discussion or argument, we become aware that our voice is raised, it is time to stop. The Jews spoke about what they called 'the sin of insult', and maintained that God does not hold anyone guiltless who speaks insultingly to another person.

In Shakespeare's *King Lear*, Lear said of Cordelia:

> Her voice was ever soft,
> Gentle and low.

It would save a great deal of heartbreak in this world if we simply learned to keep our voices down and if, when we had nothing good to say to a person, we did not say anything at all. The argument which has to be supported by shouting is no argument; and the dispute which has to be conducted through an exchange of insults is not an argument but a brawl.

So, Paul comes to the summing up of his advice. He tells us to be *kind* (*chrēstos*). The Greeks defined this quality as the attitude of mind which thinks as much of its neighbour's affairs as it does of its own. Kindness has learned the secret of looking outwards all the time, and not inwards. He tells us to forgive others as God forgave us. So, in one sentence, Paul lays down the law of personal relationships – that we should treat others as Jesus Christ has treated us.

THE IMITATION OF GOD

Ephesians 5:1–8

> You must become imitators of God, as well-loved children imitate their father. You must live in love, as Christ loved you, and gave himself to God as a sacrifice and an offering, a sacrifice which was the odour of a sweet savour to God. Let no one even mention fornication and unclean living and insatiable desire among you – it does not befit God's consecrated people to talk about things like that. Let no one even mention shameful conduct. Let there be no foolish talking and graceless jesting among you – for these things are not fitting for people like you. But rather let your talk be a

gracious thanksgiving to God. You know this and you
are well aware of it, that no fornicator, no unclean liver,
no one who is characterized by that greed – which is
idolatry – has any share in the kingdom of Christ and
God. Let no one deceive you with empty words. It is
because of these vices that the wrath of God comes upon
the children of disobedience. Don't become partners
with them.

PAUL sets before his Christian people the highest standard in
all the world; he tells them they must be imitators of God.
Later, in the second century, Clement of Alexandria was to
say daringly that the truly wise Christian practises being God.
When Paul talked of imitation, he was using language which
the wisest Greeks could understand. *Mimēsis, imitation*, was
a main part in the training of an orator. The teachers of rhetoric
declared that the learning of oratory depended on three things
– theory, imitation and practice. The main part of their training
was the study and the imitation of the masters who had gone
before. It is as if Paul said: 'If you were to train to be an
orator, you would be told to imitate those who are experts in
making speeches. Since you are training in life, you must
imitate the Lord of all good life.'

Above all, Christians must imitate the love and the forgiveness of God. Paul uses a typical Old Testament phrase,
'odour of a sweet savour', which goes back to a very old
idea, as old as sacrifice itself. When a sacrifice was offered
on an altar, the smell of the burning meat went up to heaven,
and the god to whom the sacrifice was offered was supposed
to feast upon that odour. A sacrifice which had the odour of a
sweet savour was specially pleasing and specially acceptable
to the god to whom it was offered.

Paul takes the old, time-honoured phrase – it occurs almost
fifty times in the Old Testament – and uses it of the sacrifice

that Jesus brought to God. The sacrifice of Jesus was well-pleasing to God.

What was that sacrifice? It was a life of perfect obedience to God and of perfect love to all men and women, an obedience so absolute and a love so infinite that they accepted the cross. What Paul says is: 'Imitate God. And you can do so only by loving one another with the same sacrificial love with which Jesus loved, and forgiving one another in love as God has done.'

Paul goes on to another matter. It has been said that chastity was the one new virtue which Christianity introduced into the world. It is certainly true that the ancient world regarded sexual immorality so lightly that it was no sin at all. It was the expected thing that a man should have a mistress. In places like Corinth, the great temples were staffed by hundreds of priestesses who were sacred prostitutes and whose earnings went to the upkeep of the Temple.

In his speech *Pro Caelio*, Cicero pleads: 'If there is anyone who thinks that young men should be absolutely forbidden the love of courtesans, he is indeed extremely severe. I am not able to deny the principle that he states. But he is at variance not only with the licence of what our own age allows but also with the customs and concessions of our ancestors. When indeed was this not done? When did anyone ever find fault with it? When was such permission denied? When was it that that which is now lawful was not lawful?'

The Greeks said that Solon was the first person to allow the introduction of prostitutes into Athens and then the building of brothels; and, with the profits of the new trade, a new Temple was built to Aphrodite, the goddess of love. Nothing could show the Greek point of view better than the fact that they saw nothing wrong in building a temple to the gods with the proceeds of prostitution.

When Paul put this emphasis on moral purity, he was setting a standard which the ordinary non-Christian had never dreamt of. That is why he pleads with them so earnestly and lays down his laws of purity with such stringency. We must remember the kind of society from which these Christian converts had come and the kind of society with which they were surrounded. There is nothing in all history like the moral miracle which Christianity brought about.

MAKING LIGHT OF SIN

Ephesians 5:1–8 (*contd*)

WE must note two other warnings which Paul gives.

(1) He says that these shameful sins are not even to be talked about. The Persians had a rule, so Herodotus tells us, by which 'it was not even allowed to speak such things as it was not allowed to do'. To joke about something or to make it a frequent subject of conversation is to introduce it into the mind and to bring nearer the actual doing of it. Paul warns that some things are not safe even to talk or to joke about. It is a grim commentary on human nature that many books, plays and films have had success simply because they dealt with forbidden and unpleasant things.

(2) He says that his converts must not allow themselves to be deceived with empty words. What does he mean? There were voices in the ancient world, even in the Christian Church, which taught people to think lightly of the sin of physical desires.

In the ancient world, there was a line of thought called Gnosticism. Gnosticism began from the belief that spirit alone is good and that matter is always evil. If that is the case, it follows that only spirit is to be valued and that matter must be utterly despised. Now, human beings are composed of two parts: they are *body* and *spirit*. According to this point of view, only the spirit matters; the body is of no importance whatsoever. Therefore, at least some of the Gnostics went on to argue, it does not matter what people do with their bodies. It will make no difference if they satisfy their desires to excess. Physical and sexual sin were of no importance because they were of the body and not of the spirit.

Christianity met such teaching with the contention that body and soul are equally important. God is the creator of both, Jesus Christ forever sanctified human flesh by taking it upon himself, the body is the temple of the Holy Spirit and Christianity is concerned with the salvation of the whole person, body, soul and spirit.

(3) That attack came from outside the Church; but an even more dangerous attack came from inside. There were those in the Church who distorted the doctrine of grace.

We hear the undertones of Paul's argument with them in Romans 6. Their argument ran like this. 'Do you say that God's grace is the greatest thing in all the world?' 'Yes.' 'Do you say that God's grace is wide enough to cover every sin?' 'Yes.' 'Then let us go on sinning, for God's grace can wipe out every sin. In fact, the more we sin, the more chances God's grace will have to operate.'

Christianity met that argument by insisting that grace was not only a privilege and a gift; it was a responsibility and an obligation. It was true that God's love could and would forgive; but the very fact that God loves us lays on us the obligation to deserve that love as best we can.

The gravest disservice anyone can do to someone else is to make that person take sin lightly. Paul pleaded with his converts not to be deceived with empty words which removed the horror from the idea of sin.

THE CHILDREN OF LIGHT

Ephesians 5:9–14

> For once you were darkness, but now you are light in
> the Lord. You must behave as children of the light, for
> the fruit of light consists in all benevolence and right-
> eousness and truth. You must decide what is well-
> pleasing to the Lord. You must take no share in the
> barren works of the dark. Rather you must expose them,
> for it is a shameful thing even to speak about the hidden
> things which are done in secret by such men. Whatever
> is exposed to the light is illuminated. And everything
> which is illuminated becomes light. That is why it says:
> 'Wake, O sleeper, and rise from the dead, and Christ
> will shine upon you.'

PAUL saw the non-Christian life as life in the dark, and the
Christian life as life in the light. So vividly does he wish to
put this that he does not say that those who are not Christians
are children of the dark and the Christians children of the
light; he says the non-Christians *are* dark and the Christians
are light. He has certain things to say about the light which
Jesus Christ brings to us.

(1) The light produces good fruit. It produces benevolence,
righteousness and truth. Benevolence (*agathōsunē*) is a
certain generosity of spirit. The Greeks themselves defined
righteousness (*dikaiosunē*) as 'giving to men and to God that
which is their due'. Truth (*alētheia*) is not in New Testament
thought simply an intellectual thing to be grasped with the
mind; it is moral truth, not only something to be *known* but
something to be *done*. The light which Christ brings makes
us useful citizens of this world; it makes us men and women
who never fail in duty, human or divine; it makes us strong to
do what we know is true.

(2) The light enables us to discriminate between what is well-pleasing and what is not pleasing to God. It is in the light of Christ that all motives and all actions must be tested. In the bazaars of the middle east, the shops are often simply little covered enclosures with no windows. Someone might want to buy a piece of silk or an article of beaten brass. Before buying it, the buyer takes it out to the street and holds it up to the sun, so that the light might reveal any flaws which happen to be in it. It is the Christian's duty to expose every action, every decision and every motive to the light of Christ.

(3) The light exposes whatever is evil. The best way to rid the world of any evil is to drag it into the light. As long as something is being done in secret, it goes on; but when it is taken into the light of day, it dies a natural death. The surest way to cleanse the depths of our own hearts and the practices of any society in which we happen to be involved is to expose them to the light of Christ.

(4) Finally, Paul says: 'Everything which is illuminated becomes light.' What he seems to mean is that light has in itself a cleansing quality. In our own time, we know that many diseases have been conquered simply by letting the sunlight in. The light of Christ is like that. We must never think of the light of Christ as only condemnatory; it is a healing thing too.

Paul concludes this passage with a quotation in poetry. In James Moffatt's translation, it runs:

> Wake up, O sleeper, and rise from the dead;
> So Christ will shine upon you.

Paul introduces the quotation as if everybody knew it, but no one now knows where it came from. There are certain interesting suggestions.

Almost certainly, being in the form of poetry, it is a fragment of an early Christian hymn. It may well have been part of a baptismal hymn. In the early Church, nearly all baptisms were of adults, confessing their faith as they came out of the old religion into Christianity. Perhaps these were the lines which were sung as they rose out of the water, to symbolize the passage from the dark sleep of the past life to the awakened life of the Christian way.

Alternatively, it has been suggested that these lines are part of a hymn, which was supposed to give the summons of the archangel when the last trumpet sounded over the earth. Then would come the great awakening when men and women rose from the sleep of death to receive the eternal life of Christ.

These things are speculations; but it seems certain that, when we read these lines, we are reading a fragment of one of the first hymns the Christian Church ever sang.

THE CHRISTIAN FELLOWSHIP

Ephesians 5:15–21

> Be very careful how you live. Do not live like unwise men, but like wise men. Use your time with all economy, for these are evil days. That is the reason why you must not be senseless, but you must understand what the will of God is. Do not get drunk with wine – that is profligacy – but be filled with the Spirit. Speak to each other in psalms and hymns and songs the Spirit teaches you. Let the words and the music of your praise to God come from your heart. Give thanks for all things at all times to God the Father in the name of our Lord Jesus Christ. Be subject to one another because you reverence Christ.

PAUL'S general appeal finishes with an exhortation to his converts to live like the wise. The times in which they are living are evil; they must rescue as much time as they can from the evil uses of the world.

He goes on to draw a contrast between a typical gathering in a society that worshipped the gods of Greece and Rome and a Christian gathering. The first gathering is apt to be a drunken revel. It is significant that we still use the word *symposium* for a discussion of a subject by a number of people; the Greek word *sumposion* literally means a drinking-party. A certain preacher was preaching on the text: 'Be filled with the Spirit.' He began with one startling sentence: 'You've got to fill a man with something.' Those who were not Christians found their happiness in filling themselves with wine and with worldly pleasures; Christians found their happiness in being filled with the Spirit.

From this passage, we can gather certain facts about the Christian gatherings in the early days.

(1) The early Church was a *singing church*. Its characteristic was psalms and hymns and spiritual songs; it had a happiness which made people sing.

(2) The early Church was a *thankful church*. The instinct was to give thanks for all things and in all places and at all times. John Chrysostom, the great preacher of the Church of a later day, had the curious thought that Christians could give thanks even for hell, because hell was a warning to keep them in the right way. The early Church was a thankful church because its members were still dazzled with the wonder that God's love had stooped to save them; and it was a church that gave thanks because its members had an awareness of being in the hands of God.

(3) The early Church was a church where people *honoured and respected each other*. Paul says that the reason for this

mutual honour and respect was that they reverenced Christ. They saw each other not in the light of their professions or social standing but in the light of Christ; and therefore they recognized the dignity of everyone.

THE PRECIOUS BOND

Ephesians 5:22–33

Wives, be subject to your husbands as to the Lord; for the husband is the head of the wife, even as Christ is the head of the Church, though there is this great difference, that Christ is the Saviour of the whole body. But, even allowing for this difference, even as the Church is subject to Christ, so wives must be subject to their husbands in everything. Husbands, love your wives, even as Christ loved the Church and gave himself for the Church, that by the washing of water he might purify her and consecrate her as she made confession of her faith, that he might make the Church to stand in his presence in all her glory, without any spot which soils, or any wrinkle which disfigures, or any such imperfection, but that she might be consecrated and blameless. So ought husbands to love their wives, to love them as they love their own bodies. He who loves his wife really loves himself. For no one ever hated his own flesh; rather he nourishes it and cherishes it. So Christ loves the Church because we are parts of his body. For this cause a man will leave his father and his mother and will cleave to his wife, and the two will become one flesh. This is a symbol which is very great – I mean when it is seen as a symbol of the relationship between Christ and the Church. However that may be, let each and every one of you love his wife as he loves himself, and let the wife reverence her husband.

No one reading this passage in the twenty-first century can fully realize how great it is. Throughout the years, the Christian view of marriage has come to be widely accepted. It is still recognized by the majority as the ideal, even in these permissive days. Even where practice has fallen short of that ideal, it has always been in the minds and hearts of those who live in a Christian situation. Marriage is regarded as the perfect union of body, mind and spirit between a man and a woman. But things were very different when Paul wrote. In this passage, Paul is setting down an ideal which shone with a radiant purity in an immoral world.

Let us look briefly at the situation against which Paul wrote this passage.

The Jews had a low view of women. In his morning prayer, there was a sentence in which a Jewish man gave thanks that God had not made him 'a Gentile, a slave or a woman'. In Jewish law, a woman was not a person but a thing. She had no legal rights whatsoever; she was absolutely her husband's possession to do with as he willed.

In theory, the Jews had the highest ideal of marriage. The Rabbis had their sayings. 'Every Jew must surrender his life rather than commit idolatry, murder or adultery.' 'The very altar sheds tears when a man divorces the wife of his youth.' But the fact was that, by Paul's day, divorce had become tragically easy.

The law of divorce is summarized in Deuteronomy 24:1. 'Suppose a man enters into marriage with a woman, but she does not please him because he finds something objectionable about her, and so he writes her a certificate of divorce, puts it in her hand, and sends her out of his house.' Obviously, everything turns on the interpretation of *something objectionable*. The stricter Rabbis, headed by the famous Shammai, held that the phrase meant adultery and only adultery, and declared that even if a wife was as mischievous as Queen Jezebel, a husband might not divorce her except for adultery. The more liberal Rabbis, headed by the equally famous Hillel, interpreted the phrase in the widest possible way. They said that it meant that a man might divorce his wife if she spoiled his dinner by putting too much salt in his food, if she walked in public with her head uncovered, if she talked with men in the streets, if she spoke disrespectfully of her husband's parents in her husband's hearing, if she was an argumentative woman, if she was troublesome or quarrelsome. A certain Rabbi Akiba interpreted the phrase *but she does not please him* to mean that a husband might divorce his wife if he found a woman whom he considered more attractive. It is easy to see which school of thought would predominate.

Two facts in Jewish law made the matter worse. First, the wife had no rights of divorce at all, unless her husband became a leper or rejected the faith or engaged in a disgusting trade such as that of a tanner. Broadly speaking, a husband, under Jewish law, could divorce his wife on any grounds, whereas there were no grounds on which a wife could divorce her husband. Second, the process of divorce was disastrously easy. The Mosaic law said that a man who wanted a divorce had to hand his wife a bill of divorce which said: 'Let this be from me your writ of divorce and letter of dismissal and deed of liberation, that you may marry whatsoever man you will.' All a man had to do was to hand that bill of divorce, correctly written out by a Rabbi, to his wife in the presence of two witnesses and the divorce was complete. The only other condition was that the woman's dowry must be returned.

At the time of Christ's coming, the marriage bond was in grave danger even among the Jews, since Jewish girls were refusing to marry because their position as a wife was so uncertain.

THE PRECIOUS BOND

Ephesians 5:22–33 (*contd*)

THE situation was worse in the Greek world. Prostitution was an essential part of Greek life. The Athenian orator and statesman Demosthenes had laid it down as the accepted rule of life: 'We have courtesans for the sake of pleasure; we have concubines for the sake of daily cohabitation; we have wives for the purpose of having children legitimately and of having a faithful guardian for all our household affairs.' The women of the respectable classes in Greece led completely secluded lives. They took no part in public life; they never appeared on the streets alone; they never even appeared at meals or at social occasions; they had their own apartments where none but their husbands might enter. It was the aim that, as the historian Xenophon had it, they 'might see as little as possible, hear as little as possible and ask as little as possible'.

The respectable woman of Greek society was brought up in such a way that companionship and fellowship in marriage was impossible. Socrates said: 'Is there anyone to whom you entrust more serious matters than to your wife – and is there anyone to whom you talk less?' Verus was the imperial colleague of the great emperor Marcus Aurelius. He was blamed by his wife for associating with other women, and his answer was that she must remember that the name of wife was a title of dignity but not of pleasure. The Greeks expected their wives to run the home and to care for their legitimate children; but they found their pleasure and their companionship elsewhere.

To make matters worse, there was no legal procedure of divorce in Greece. As someone has put it, divorce was by nothing else than caprice, the result of a whim. The one security that a wife had was that her dowry must be returned. Home and family life were near to being extinct, and faithfulness was completely non-existent.

THE PRECIOUS BOND

Ephesians 5:22–33 (*contd*)

In Rome, the matter was still worse; its degeneracy was tragic. For the first 500 years of the Roman Republic, there had not been one single case of divorce. The first recorded divorce was that of Spurius Carvilius Ruga in 234 BC. But, at the time of Paul, Roman family life was in ruins. The philosopher Seneca writes that women were married to be divorced and divorced to be married. In Rome, the Romans did not commonly date their years by numbers; they called them by the names of the consuls. Seneca says that women dated the years by the names of their husbands. The poet Martial tells of a woman who had had ten husbands; Juvenal, who was a lawyer, tells of one who had had eight husbands in five years. The biblical scholar Jerome declares it to be true that in Rome there was a woman who was married to her twenty-third husband and she herself was his twenty-first wife. We find a Roman emperor, Augustus, demanding that the husband of the Lady Livia should divorce her when she was pregnant so that he might marry her himself. We find even Cicero, in his old age, putting away his wife Terentia so that he might marry a young heiress, whose trustee he was, and thereby acquire her estate in order to pay his debts.

That is not to say that there was no such thing as faithfulness. The historian Suetonius tells of a Roman lady called Mallonia who committed suicide rather than submit to the favours of the emperor Tiberius. But it is not too much to say that the whole atmosphere was adulterous. The marriage bond was on the way to complete breakdown.

It is against this background that Paul writes. When he wrote this lovely passage, he was not stating a view that everyone held. He was calling men and women to a new purity and a new fellowship in the married life. It is impossible to exaggerate the cleansing effect that Christianity had on home life in the ancient world and the benefits it brought to women.

THE GROWTH OF PAUL'S THOUGHT

Ephesians 5:22–33 (*contd*)

IN this passage, we find Paul's real thinking on marriage. There are things which Paul wrote about marriage which puzzle us and may make us wish that he had never written them. The unfortunate thing is that it is these things that are so often quoted as Paul's view of marriage.

One of the strangest chapters is 1 Corinthians 7. He is talking about marriage and about the relationships between men and women. The blunt truth is that Paul's teaching is that marriage is permissible merely in order to avoid something worse. 'Because of cases of sexual immorality,' he writes, 'each man should have his own wife and each woman her own husband' (1 Corinthians 7:2). He allows that a widow may marry again, but it would be better if she remained single (1 Corinthians 7:39–40). He would prefer the unmarried and the widows not to marry. 'But if they are not practising self-control, they should marry. For it is better to marry than to be aflame with passion' (1 Corinthians 7:9).

There was a reason why Paul wrote like that. It was because he expected the second coming of Jesus at any time. It was therefore his conviction that no one should undertake any earthly ties whatsoever, but that all should concentrate on using the short time which remained in preparing for the coming of their Lord. 'The unmarried man is anxious about the affairs of the Lord, how to please the Lord; but the married man is anxious about the affairs of the world, how to please his wife' (1 Corinthians 7:32–3).

Between 1 Corinthians and Ephesians, there is a space of perhaps nine years. In these nine years, Paul had realized that the second coming was not to be as soon as he had thought – that in fact he and his people were living not in a temporary situation but in a more or less permanent situation. And it is in Ephesians that we find Paul's true teaching on marriage, that Christian marriage is the most precious relationship in life, whose only parallel is the relationship between Christ and the Church.

It is just possible that the Corinthians passage was coloured by Paul's personal experience. It would seem that, in his days as a zealous Jew, he was a member of the Sanhedrin. When he is telling of his conduct towards the Christians, he says: 'I also cast my vote against them' (Acts 26:10). It would also seem that one of the qualifications for membership of the Sanhedrin was marriage, and that therefore Paul must have been a married man. He never mentions his wife. Why? It may well be that it was because she turned against him when he became a Christian. It may be that, when he wrote 1 Corinthians, Paul was speaking out of a situation in which he not only expected the immediate coming of Christ but had also found his own marriage one of his greatest problems and deepest heartbreaks – so that he saw marriage as a handicap for Christians.

THE BASIS OF LOVE

Ephesians 5:22–33 (*contd*)

SOMETIMES, the emphasis of this passage is entirely misplaced, and it is read as if its essence was the subordination of wife to husband. The single phrase, 'The husband is the head of the wife', is quoted in isolation. But the basis of the passage is not control; it is love. Paul says certain things about the love that a husband must have for his wife.

(1) It must be a *sacrificial* love. He must love her as Christ loved the Church and gave himself for the Church. It must never be a selfish love. Christ loved the Church, not that the Church might do things for him, but that he might do things for the Church. The fourth-century Church father John Chrysostom has a wonderful expansion of this passage: 'Hast thou seen the measure of obedience? Hear also the measure of love. Wouldst thou that thy wife shouldst obey thee as the Church doth Christ? Have care thyself for her as Christ for the Church. And if it be needful that thou shouldst give thy life for her, or be cut to pieces a thousand times, or endure anything whatever, refuse it not . . . He brought the Church to his feet by his great care, not by threats nor fear nor any such thing; so do thou conduct thyself towards thy wife.'

The husband is head of the wife – true, Paul said that; but he also said that the husband must love the wife as Christ loved the Church, with a love which never exercises a tyranny of control but which is ready to make any sacrifice for her good.

(2) It must be a *purifying* love. Christ cleansed and consecrated the Church by the washing with water on the day when each member of the Church made a personal confession of faith. It may well be that Paul has in mind a

Greek custom. One of the Greek marriage customs was that, before the bride was taken to her marriage, she was bathed in the water of a stream sacred to some god or goddess. In Athens, for instance, the bride was bathed in the waters of the Callirhoe, which was sacred to the goddess Athene. It is of baptism that Paul is thinking. By the washing of baptism and by the confession of faith, Christ sought to make for himself a Church, cleansed and consecrated, until there was neither soiling spot nor disfiguring wrinkle upon it. Any love which drags a person down is false. Any love which coarsens instead of refining the character, which necessitates deceit, which weakens the moral strength, is not love. Real love is the great purifier of life.

(3) It must be a *caring* love. A man must love his wife as he loves his own body. Real love loves not to extract service, nor to ensure that its own physical comfort is attended to; it cherishes the one it loves. There is something very wrong when a man regards his wife, consciously or unconsciously, as simply the one who cooks his meals and washes his clothes and cleans his house and brings up his children.

(4) It is an *unbreakable* love. For the sake of this love, a man leaves father and mother and is joined to his wife. They become one flesh. He is as united to her as the members of the body are united to each other, and would no more think of separating from her than of tearing his own body apart. Here indeed was an ideal in an age when men and women changed partners with as little thought as they changed clothes.

(5) The whole relationship is *in the Lord*. In the Christian home, Jesus is an always-remembered, though an unseen, guest. In Christian marriage, there are not two partners, but three – and the third is Christ.

CHILDREN AND PARENTS

Ephesians 6:1–4

> Children, obey your parents, as Christian children
> should. Honour your father and your mother – for this
> is the first commandment to which a promise is attached
> – that it may be well with you, and that you may live
> long on the earth. Fathers, do not move your children to
> anger, but bring them up in the discipline and the
> admonition of the Lord.

IF the Christian faith did a great deal for women, it did even
more for children. In Roman civilization contemporary with
Paul, there existed certain features which made life dangerous
for children.

(1) There was the Roman *patria potestas*, the father's
power. Under the *patria potestas*, a Roman father had absolute
power over his family. He could sell them as slaves; he could
make them work in his fields even in chains; he could punish
as he liked and could even inflict the death penalty. Further,
the power of the Roman father extended over a child's whole
life, as long as the father lived. A Roman son never came of
age. Even when he was a grown man, even if he were a
magistrate of the city, even if the state had crowned him with
well-deserved honours, he remained within his father's
absolute power. 'The great mistake', writes the classical
archaeologist Wilhelm Adolf Becker, 'consisted in the Roman
father considering the power which Nature imposes as a duty
on the elders, of guiding and protecting a child during infancy,
as extending over his freedom, involving his life and death,
and continuing over his entire existence.' It is true that the
father's power was seldom carried to its limits, because public
opinion would not have allowed it; but the fact remains that,

in the time of Paul, children were absolutely in their father's power.

(2) There was the custom of child exposure. When a child was born, it was placed at its father's feet; and, if the father stooped and lifted the child, that meant that he acknowledged it and wanted to keep it. If he turned and walked away, it meant that he refused to acknowledge it, and the child could quite literally be thrown out.

There is a letter whose date is I BC from a man called Hilarion to his wife Alis. He has gone to Alexandria, and he writes home on domestic affairs:

> Hilarion to Alis his wife heartiest greetings, and to my dear Berous and Apollonarion. Know that we are still even now in Alexandria. Do not worry if when all others return I remain in Alexandria. I beg and beseech of you to take care of the little child, and, as soon as we receive wages, I will send them to you. If – good luck to you! – you have a child, if it is a boy, let it live; if it is a girl, throw it out. You told Aphrodisias to tell me: 'Do not forget me.' How can I forget you? I beg you therefore not to worry.

It is a strange letter, so full of affection and yet so callous towards the child who may be born.

A Roman baby always ran the risk of being rejected and exposed. In the time of Paul, that risk was even greater. We have seen how the marriage bond had collapsed and how men and women changed their partners with bewildering rapidity. Under such circumstances, a child was a misfortune. So few children were born that the Roman government actually passed legislation that the amount of any legacy that a childless couple could receive was limited. It was the custom that unwanted children were left in the Roman forum. There they became the property of anyone who cared to pick them up. They were collected at night by people who looked after them in order to sell them as slaves or to stock the brothels of Rome.

(3) Ancient civilization was merciless to the sickly or deformed child. Seneca writes: 'We slaughter a fierce ox; we strangle a mad dog; we plunge the knife into sickly cattle lest they taint the herd; children who are born weakly and deformed we drown.' Children who were weak or imperfectly formed had little hope of survival.

It was against this situation that Paul wrote his advice to children and parents. If ever we are asked what good Christianity has done to the world, we need only point to the change brought about in the status of women and of children.

CHILDREN AND PARENTS

Ephesians 6:1–4 (*contd*)

PAUL tells children that they should obey the commandment and honour their parents. He says this is the *first* commandment. He probably means that it was the first commandment which Christian children were taught to memorize. The honour Paul demands is not the honour of mere lip-service. The way to honour parents is to obey them, to respect them, and never to cause them pain.

Paul sees that there is another side to the question. He tells fathers that they must not provoke their children to anger. The eighteenth-century German commentator Johann Bengel, considering why this command is so definitely addressed to *fathers*, says that mothers have a kind of divine patience but 'fathers are more liable to be carried away by wrath'.

It is a strange thing that Paul repeats this command even more fully in Colossians 3:21. 'Fathers,' he says, 'do not provoke your children, *or they may lose heart.*' Bengel says that the plague of youth is a 'broken spirit', discouraged by continuous criticism and rebuke and discipline that is too strict. The theologian David Smith thinks that Paul wrote out of bitter personal experience. He writes: 'There is here a quivering note of personal emotion, and it seems as though the heart of the aged captive had been reverting to the past and recalling the loveless years of his own childhood. Nurtured in the austere atmosphere of traditional orthodoxy, he had experienced scant tenderness and much severity, and had known that "plague of youth, a broken spirit".'

There are three ways in which we can do injustice to our children.

(1) We can forget that things do change and that the customs of one generation are not the customs of another. The short-story writer Elinor Mordaunt tells how once she stopped her little daughter from doing something by saying: 'I was never allowed to do that when I was your age.' And the child answered: 'But you must remember, mother, that you were *then*, and I'm *now*.'

(2) We can exercise such a control that it is an insult to the way we bring up our children. To keep children reined in for too long is to say that we do not trust them, which is simply to say that we have no confidence in the way in which we have trained them. It is better to make the mistake of too much trust than of too much control.

(3) We can forget the duty of encouragement. Martin Luther's father was very strict, strict to the point of cruelty. Luther used to say: 'Spare the rod and spoil the child – that is true; but beside the rod keep an apple to give him when he has done well.' The eighteenth-century artist Benjamin

West tells how he became a painter. One day, his mother went out leaving him in charge of his little sister Sally. In his mother's absence, he discovered some bottles of coloured ink and began to paint Sally's portrait. In doing so, he made a considerable mess of things with ink blots everywhere. His mother came back. She saw the mess but said nothing. She picked up the piece of paper and saw the drawing. 'Why,' she said, 'it's Sally!' and she stooped and kissed him. Afterwards, Benjamin West always used to say: 'My mother's kiss made me a painter.' Encouragement did more than rebuke could ever do. The novelist Anna Buchan tells how her grandmother had a favourite phrase even when she was very old: 'Never daunton [discourage] youth.'

As Paul sees it, children must honour their parents, and parents must never discourage their children.

MASTERS AND SLAVES

Ephesians 6:5–9

> Slaves, obey your human masters with fear and trembling, in sincerity of heart, as you would Christ himself. Do not work only when you are being watched. Do not work only to satisfy men. But work as the slave of Christ, doing God's will heartily. Let your service be given with goodwill, as to Christ and not to men. Be well assured that each of us, whether he is slave or free, will be rewarded by the Lord for whatever good we have done. And you masters, act in the same way towards your slaves. Have done with threats. For you well know that they and you have a Master in heaven, and with him there is no respect of persons.

WHEN Paul wrote to slaves in the Christian Church, he must have been writing to a very large number.

It has been computed that in the Roman Empire there were 60,000,000 slaves. In Paul's day, a kind of terrible idleness had fallen on the citizens of Rome. Rome was ruler of the world, and therefore it was beneath the dignity of a Roman citizen to work. Practically all work was done by slaves. Even doctors and teachers, even the closest friends of the emperors, their secretaries who dealt with letters and appeals and finance, were slaves.

Often, there were bonds of the deepest loyalty and affection between master and slave. Pliny 'the Younger' writes to a friend that he is deeply affected because some of his well-loved slaves have died. He has two consolations, although they are not enough to comfort his grief. 'I have always very readily manumitted [released] my slaves (for their death does not seem altogether untimely, if they have lived long enough to receive their freedom); the other, that I have allowed them to make a kind of will, which I observe as rigidly as if it were good in law.' There the kindly master speaks.

But basically the life of the slave was grim and terrible. In law, slaves were not people but *things*. Aristotle lays it down that there can never be friendship between master and slave, for they have nothing in common – 'for a slave is a living tool, just as a tool is an inanimate slave'. The Roman scholar Varro, writing on agriculture, divides agricultural instruments into three classes – the articulate, the inarticulate and the mute. The articulate comprises the slaves, the inarticulate the cattle, and the mute the vehicles. A slave is no better than an animal that happens to be able to talk. The statesman Cato 'the Elder' gives advice to a man taking over a farm. He must go over it and throw out everything that is past its best and no longer of use; and old slaves too must be thrown out on the scrap heap to starve. When slaves are ill, it is sheer extravagance to issue them with normal rations.

The law was quite clear. Gaius, the Roman lawyer, in the *Institutes* lays it down: 'We may note that it is universally accepted that the master possesses the power of life and death over the slave.' If a slave ran away, at best the penalty was to be branded on the forehead with the letter F for *fugitivus*, which means runaway; at worst, the punishment was death. The terror of slaves was that they were absolutely at the mercy of the master's whims. Augustus crucified a slave because he killed a pet quail.

Juvenal tells of a Roman woman who ordered a slave to be killed for no other reason than that she lost her temper with him. When her husband protested, she said: 'You call a slave a man, do you? He has done no wrong, you say? Be it so; it is my will and my command; let my will be the voucher for the deed.'

The female slaves who served their mistresses within the household often had their hair torn out and their cheeks scratched by their mistresses' nails. Juvenal tells of the master 'who delights in the sound of a cruel flogging think-ing it sweeter than any siren's song'. Or 'who revels in clanking chains', or 'who summons a torturer and brands the slave because a couple of towels are lost'. Another Roman writer lays it down: 'Whatever a master does to a slave, undeservedly, in anger, willingly, unwillingly, in forgetful-ness, after careful thought, knowingly, unknowingly, is judgment, justice and law.'

It is against this terrible background that Paul's advice to slaves must be read.

MASTERS AND SLAVES

Ephesians 6:5–9 (*contd*)

PAUL'S advice to slaves provides us with the gospel of Christian work.

(1) He does not tell them to rebel; he tells them to be Christian where they are. The great message of Christianity to everyone is that it is where God has placed us that we must live out the Christian life. The circumstances may be all against us, but that only makes the challenge greater. Christianity does not offer us an escape from circumstances; it offers us the ability to conquer circumstances.

(2) He tells the slaves that work must be done well not only when the overseer's eye is on them; it must be done in the awareness that God's eye is on them. Every single piece of work a Christian produces must be good enough to show to God. The problem that the world has always faced and that it faces acutely today is basically not economic but religious. We can never make people do their jobs better simply by improving conditions or offering better rewards. It is a Christian duty to see to these things; but in themselves they will never produce good work. Still less will we produce good work by increasing oversight and multiplying punishments. The secret of good work is to do it for God.

Paul has something to say to those who are in charge of others, too. They must remember that, although they are in charge, they are still the servants of God. They too must remember that all that they do is done in the sight of God. Above all, they must remember that the day comes when they and those for whom they are responsible will stand before God; and then status in the world will no longer be relevant.

The problem of work would be solved if workers and employers alike would take their orders from God.

THE ARMOUR OF GOD

Ephesians 6:10–20

> Finally, be strong in the Lord and in the power of his strength. Put on the armour of God, so that you may be able to stand against the devices of the devil. It is not with blood and flesh you have to wrestle, but against powers and against authorities, against the world rulers of this darkness, against malicious spiritual forces in the heavenly places. Because of this, you must take the armour of God that you may be able to stand against them in the evil day, and that you may be able to stand fast, after you have done all things which are your duty. Stand with truth as a belt about your waist. Put on righteousness as a breastplate. Have your feet shod with readiness to preach the gospel of peace. In all things, take faith as a shield, for with it you will be able to quench the flaming darts of the evil one. Put on the helmet of salvation. Take the sword of the Spirit, which is the word of God. Keep praying in the Spirit at every crisis with every kind of prayer and entreaty to God. To that end, be sleepless in your persevering prayer for all God's consecrated people. Pray for me that I may be allowed to speak with open mouth, and boldly to make known the secret of the gospel, for which I am an envoy in a chain. Pray that I may have freedom to declare it, as I ought to speak.

As Paul takes leave of his people, he thinks of the greatness of the struggle which lies before them. Undoubtedly, life was much more terrifying for the people of those times than it is for us today. They believed implicitly in evil spirits, which filled the air and were determined to bring harm to people. The words which Paul uses – powers, authorities, world rulers – are all names for different classes of these evil spirits. To him, the whole universe was a battle ground. Christians not only had to contend with the attacks from other people; they had to contend with the attacks of spiritual forces that were fighting against God. We may not take Paul's actual language literally; but our experience will tell us that there is an active power of evil in the world. The writer Robert Louis Stevenson once said: 'You know the Caledonian Railway Station in Edinburgh? One cold, east windy morning, I met Satan there.' We do not know what actually happened to Stevenson, but we recognize the experience; we have all felt the force of that evil influence which seeks to make us sin.

Paul suddenly sees a picture staring him in the face. All this time, he was chained by the wrist to a Roman soldier. Night and day, a soldier was there to ensure that he would not escape. Paul was literally an ambassador in chains. Now, he was the kind of man who could get along with anyone; and without a doubt he had often talked to the soldiers who were compelled to be so near him. As he writes, the soldier's armour suggests a picture to him. Christians too have armour; and item by item Paul takes the armour of the Roman soldier and translates it into Christian terms.

There is the belt of truth. It was the belt which went round the soldier's tunic and from which his sword hung and which gave him freedom of movement. Others may guess and feel their way; Christians move freely and quickly because they know the truth.

There is the breastplate of righteousness. When we are clothed in righteousness, we are impregnable. Words are no defence against accusations, but a good life is. Once, a man accused Plato of certain crimes. 'Well then,' said Plato, 'we must live in such a way as to prove that his accusations are a lie.' The only way to meet the accusations against Christianity is to show how good a Christian can be.

There are the sandals. Sandals were the sign of one equipped and ready to move. The sign of Christians is that they are eager to be on the way to share the gospel with others who have not heard it.

There is the shield. The word Paul uses is not that for the comparatively small round shield; it is the word used for the great oblong shield which the heavily armed warrior wore. One of the most dangerous weapons in ancient warfare was the fiery dart. It was a dart tipped with fibres of rope dipped in pitch. The pitch-soaked rope was set alight and the dart was thrown. The great oblong shield was made of two sections of wood, glued together. When the shield was presented to the dart, the dart sank into the wood and the flame was put out. Faith can deal with the darts of temptation. For Paul, faith is always complete trust in Christ. When we walk closely with Christ, we are safe from temptation.

There is salvation for a helmet. Salvation is not something which only looks back. The salvation which is in Christ gives us forgiveness for the sins of the past and strength to conquer sin in the days to come.

There is the sword; and the sword is the word of God. The word of God is both our weapon of defence against sin and our weapon of attack against the sins of the world. During the English Civil War, Oliver Cromwell's Ironsides fought with a sword in one hand and a Bible in the other. We can never win God's battles without God's book.

Finally, Paul comes to the greatest weapon of all – and that is prayer. We note three things that he says about prayer. (1) It must be constant. Our tendency is so often to pray only in the great crises of life; but it is from daily prayer that Christians will find daily strength. (2) It must be intense. Unfocused prayer never got anyone anywhere. Prayer demands the concentration of every faculty upon God. (3) It must be unselfish. The Jews had a saying: 'Let a man unite himself with the community in his prayers.' Often, our prayers are too much for ourselves and too little for others. We must learn to pray as much for others and with others as for ourselves.

Finally, Paul asks for the prayers of his friends for himself. And he asks not for comfort or for peace but that he may yet be allowed to proclaim God's secret, that his love is for all men and women. We do well to remember that all Christian leaders and all Christian preachers need their people to hold up their hands in prayer.

THE FINAL BLESSING

Ephesians 6:21–4

> Tychicus, the beloved brother and faithful servant in the Lord, will provide you with all information, that you too may know how things are going with me, how I do. That is the very reason that I sent him to you, that you may know my affairs and that he may encourage your hearts.
>
> Peace be to the brethren, and love with faith, from God the Father and from the Lord Jesus Christ. Grace be with all who love the Lord Jesus with a love which defies death.

As we have seen, the letter to the Ephesians was a circular letter, and the one who took it from church to church was Tychicus. Unlike most of his letters, Ephesians gives us no personal information about Paul, except that he was in prison; but Tychicus, as he went from church to church, would tell how Paul was getting on and would convey a message of personal encouragement.

Paul finishes with a blessing – and in it all the great words come again. The peace which was a person's highest good, the faith which was complete resting in Christ, the grace which was the lovely free gift of God – these things Paul calls from God upon his friends. Above all, he prays for love, that they may know the love of God, that they may love one another as God loves them, and that they may love Jesus Christ with an undying love.